I0437502

JUS IN BELLO
(Conduct of War)

A Pamphlet
On Government and War

By

Thomas M. Bates

authorHOUSE®

AuthorHouse™
1663 Liberty Drive, Suite 200
Bloomington, IN 47403
www.authorhouse.com
Phone: 1-800-839-8640

© 2008 Thomas M. Bates. All rights reserved.
No part of this book may be reproduced, stored in a retrieval system, or
transmitted by any means without the written permission of the author.
First published by AuthorHouse 11/5/2008

ISBN:978-1-4389-2295-9 (sc)
ISBN:978-1-4389-2296-6 (hc)

Printed in the United States of America
Bloomington, Indiana
This book is printed on acid-free paper.

Library of Congress Control Number: 2008909107

"…to petition the Government for a redress of grievances."

Table of Contents

A Prefatory Comment 1
On Attacks On Rights To Privacy 15
On Bureaucracies 19
On Bush Rhetoric 23
On The Surge 27
On High Rank Muddling 31
On Redirecting Resources 35
More On Resource Allocation 41
On The Walter Reed Hospital Debacle 45
On Accountability 49
On The Attorney General 53
On Blackwater 57
On Virginia Tech 63
On Gun Control 65
On Dog Days Of Summer 2007 69
On The Iraq War 73
On Combat Security Contractors 77
On Indigenous Security Forces 83
On The Iraq War Is Not The War! 87
On Financial Solutions 91
On The United States Army 95
On The United States Marines 99
On The United States Air Force 103
On The United States Navy 109
On Jus In Bello 113
"Right" Judgment; Flawed Logic; Shoddy Historiography 121
A Note To The Extremist Right 141

A Prefatory Comment

    This book is a series of real-time essays composed during the last two years of the Bush Administration. The source of my motivation emanated from a letter that I wrote to the Republican National Committee in 2004 to convince them that I was very dissatisfied with the direction that the country was moving and that I would not vote the Republican ticket in the national election and to drop me from the party's mailing list. In 2006 in the throes of the Congressional elections I started receiving the Republican mailings again. When the Democrats gained limited control of the congress and the country was still on the "stay the course" mantra, I started this series of essays, mostly in letter form, addressed to the Democratic National Committee for their review and use during the next several months until the 2008 elections. Of course, I had no idea at the time that this primary season would turn out to cover nearly the entire period of the congressional session.

    Another motivation for me was to thoroughly understand the issues. I felt that if I could put some of my thoughts on paper, I might be able to more fully understand the positions of the left and the right of current American politics. I could put down my "two cents worth" and see how it melds with the talking heads and the candidates. At the very least these written thoughts might reduce my personal frustration due to an apparent deviation from policies, freedoms and moralities that I had come to accept over a lifetime as an American citizen. Unfortunately, this motivation only exacerbated my frustration, although I did see some sanity seep into the Bush Administration when the negativisms in the domestic public and the international community grew to

1

such an astounding crescendo. But this administration's baby step toward rationality may have been too little; too late. The first six years of this administration perpetrated an unabashed imperialistic, preemptive aggression on another sovereign nation-state, based on faulty intelligence while the legitimate target for our wrath was left to rejuvenate itself. This powerful transnational organization is again back to strength and very possibly more dangerous than it was before 9/11. During this time the administration's economic policies imposed a crushing deficit on the populace and inflated the national debt by seventy per cent. Our military, the envy of the world before March 2003, now lays prostrate, exhausted after six years of war. Our allies of years past have bid their political farewell because of our aggressive behavior. Meanwhile, time honored American freedoms were eroded in the interest of perceived increased safety.

Ronald Reagan often referred to John Winthrop's vision of "a shining city upon a hill" as a beacon for the rest of the world to follow out of a darkness of oppression. In his farewell address in January 1989, the "Great Communicator" said:

> *"I've spoken of the shining city all my political life, but I don't know if I ever quite communicated what I saw when I said it. But in my mind it was a tall proud city built on rocks stronger than oceans, wind-swept, ...teeming with people of all kinds living in harmony and peace, a city with free ports that hummed with commerce and creativity, and if there had to be city walls, the walls had doors and the doors were open to anyone with the will and the heart to get there."*

> *"...but more than that; after 200 years, two centuries, she still stands strong and true.... And she's still a beacon, still a magnet for all who must have freedom...."*

President Reagan, the quintessential optimist, had a beautiful fantasy transfixed in his mind. Today, nearly twenty years later, his magnificent thought has been sullied by greed, corruption and poor judgment. The Gipper's optimism didn't contemplate these recent fissures of the last seven and a half years under the "rocks stronger than oceans"; his foresight didn't envisage the dangers that lurked on the slippery slopes to the left and to the right of the hill supporting this shining city of freedom and democracy. His naiveté didn't grasp the impact of extremism that shifts freedom's bright beacon to the verge of an abyss. If this city's shift is too far to the left, then Reagan's vision slides down a very steep slippery slope to socialism; then communism; then totalitarianism. If the shining beacon shifts too far to the right, then the Gipper's beautiful dream slides down the slippery slope to fascism; then National Socialism; then ultimately despotism. In either direction that we stumble, the result is the same, the obliteration of the Great American Experiment. It is for us, this current generation, to stabilize the shining city; to mend the fissures under the rocks that widen the center aisle in congress and to close the divisive schism between the reds and blues, the conservatives and liberals. Disagreement and debate are essential, but mutual respect and ultimate compromise from the best ideas from left *and* right will stabilize this fragile prescience.

In the last seven and a half years, we have seen our "shining city upon the hill" inch to the right. (Mind you, it has inched to the left from time to time in our history too.) Our beloved country has not slipped over the precipice yet, but it has descended into a murky slough of policies that include deficit spending, corruption, privileged no-bid contracting, bureaucratic incompetence, torture of prisoners, deception of the American public and foreign allies, disingenuous spin on major issues, character assassination, innuendos, dirty political tricks, obsessive secrecy, invasion of privacy, loss of privilege of habeas corpus and fear mongering; all in the interest to establish a permanent majority political party. The result has not made the American people safer, healthier, happier or wealthier; the result has made the American people less free! As conscientious citizens we cannot permit this to happen. We must be ever vigilant!

The reader may notice that the numbers and statistics change, sometimes substantially, over the course of the readings. This, of course, is due to the time lapse from the first essays to the last. During this time period many more soldiers, Marines and innocent noncombatants were killed and wounded. In addition, more accurate data became available over the time based on more thorough analysis. Also since these essays were written in real-time from only unclassified resources and without privileged access to the powers in government, some of my opinions and observations have proved to be off the mark (or as Justice Scalia might brusquely admonish, "Dead wrong!") while others have continued to have merit. That's fine with me, because it shows

Thomas M. Bates

that I'm no political soothsayer or clairvoyant. I am only Joe Ordinary, a concerned citizen. Enjoy my thoughts and use them as a catalyst for your own. Disagreement is as important as agreement. Think hard about our great gift of American freedoms that we must defend from our enemies abroad as well as our own selves at home.

October 18, 2004

Mr. Mike Retzer
Treasurer
Republican National Committee
310 First Street, Southeast
Washington, D.C. 20003

Dear Mr. Retzer:

I received your letter soliciting my contribution to the RNC last week. In this communication I will try to answer your questions regarding my non-participation in the Republican Party as best that I can. I have not done my part to support President Bush and the Republican Party because I am a Democrat and have never contributed to your party. (Please review the letter that I sent to the GOP during the 2002 campaigns. I have voted for the Republican Nominee on only two occasions in over forty years.) Your information that I have generously supported the Republican Party over the years is incorrect.

I applaud the fact that this country has a Democratic ticket in 2004 that has the possibility of removing this administration from power on November 2. However, I have to say that I have great respect for many Republicans such as Colin Powell, John McCain, John Werner, Richard Lugar, Arnold Schwarzenegger, and Robert and Elizabeth Dole to name only a few. Peeking back in history, I have admired such men as Berry Goldwater, Everett Dirksen, Robert Taft, Dwight Eisenhower, Howard Taft, Theodore Roosevelt, and, of course, A. Lincoln. Additionally, I think that George H. W. Bush did a good job in general, specifically in foreign policy during his four years in the White House. His total lifetime service to this country certainly qualifies him as a National Treasure. As president he handled his Iraqi war with great craft in diplomacy to bring together a true coalition to stifle the aggressive behavior of Saddam Hussein when he invaded his neighboring sovereign nation-state of Kuwait. As you recall the coalition ousted this tyrant from Kuwait and sent him packing at huge loss to his military. There was no attempt on the part of this coalition to invade and occupy Iraq. The coalition was not only designed to punish aggression but also to respect the nation-state system as it has been operative for the last five hundred years. This was, in my opinion, a *responsible* military response to an international crisis. President G.H.W. Bush's only mistake however, and it was no small one, came after the war. In my opinion, his encouragement for the Shiite Muslims in the Southern Region to rise up against the tyranny of the Sunni Muslims in the Iraqi government was ill advised. President G.H.W. Bush was forced politically to withdraw the United States' material and moral support that was essential for the Shiites to be successful and left them to suffer greatly. This was a travesty!

On the other hand in the present administration, President George W. Bush and his close advisors, such as Vice-President Cheney, Karl Rove, and Secretary Donald Rumsfeld have not met my standards as national leaders, diplomatists and advisors. Let me take a moment to list some of my concerns about the way that this administration has erred in their duties and responsibilities to the people of this country and the people in the community of nations.

First of all, I think that the initial response of the 43rd Administration to the 9/11 attack on the United States was appropriate. We identified the source of the attack quickly through some good intelligence and diplomatic expertise. We placed Special Forces units on the ground in a very short time. We allied with the Northern Alliance, supplied materials and rapidly moved on the offensive against the culpable al Qaeda and their sheltering Taliban allies. We destroyed the egregious Taliban and put the al Qaeda hierarchy on the run. This was a good thing. But just as we were in the process of pursuing the terrorist's leadership, and were about to finalize this adequate response to the outrageous crimes of 9/11 against the United States, the 43rd administration refocused on Iraq! Why did they do this? Some of the official reasons were: 1) Saddam was supporting the al Qaeda terrorist movement; 2) the Iraqi government had stockpiles of WMD and were about to attack surrounding countries and the United States; 3) Saddam had been killing the Kurds in the northern regions; 4) Saddam had tried to assassinate George H.W. Bush several years before.

Unfortunately for the administration, in their efforts to justify the invasion of Iraq, the first two reasons were *not* true. If the administration had had the patience to wait for the final results of the international inspectors, perhaps we would have known the truth before over one-thousand of our young people were dead, nearly six-thousand maimed and $120 billion wasted. For the third reason listed, although evidence is strong that Hussein murdered thousands of Kurds in the northern region, there is also evidence that these people were contriving a revolt against the Sunni regime in Baghdad. Under international protocol Saddam Hussein exercised his authority as a head of state and initiated a pre-emptive strike against this perceived internal enemy. This action is not without precedent in world history. The fourth reason, the assassination attempt on our 41st President, was certainly an outrageous affront against an American icon and the people of the United States. But attempts on the life of our presidents happen. Four have been successful over the years. There have been other failed attempts on the lives of our presidents. (Truman was attacked by separatist Puerto Ricans, Ford by some misguided leftists and Reagan by a mentally disturbed young man.) Most attempts have been perpetrated by members of our own citizenry. This criminal act is indescribably awful, but assassination is not a cause for war. (I can't speak for George H.W. Bush, but if I were an ex-president and the nation sent thousands of youngsters to their deaths to avenge an attempt on my life, I would be appalled! And I would work with all my resources to prevent it.) We all have to remember that the Office of President of the United States is a risky job and subject to personal violent attack. But does this justify a pre-emptive strike/regime change?

The result of the refocus of our military aggression toward Iraq has left the real war on terror in limbo and has seriously damaged the United States' image abroad with its aggressive policy against Iraq during the last three years. The 43rd administration has consistently demonstrated shortsighted vision in international relations and reckless analysis of available intelligence in the war against terror. As mentioned above, the evidence is very strong that Iraq was not supporting al Qaeda. As a result, in the eyes of many around the world, the United States has invaded another sovereign nation-state without good cause. When attempts by the community of nations tried to prevent this aggression and point out this rash policy to the 43rd administration, the administration condescended to them and belittled their sage advice.

Our allies have argued for a more rational approach to the dangers perpetrated by the stateless terrorist organizations. But this administration turns a blind eye to their suggestions and insists on violating the sovereign borders of Iraq with the excuse that it posed a serious threat to our most vital national interest. This has turned out not to be the case. Also, this administration has adopted as policy the protocol of pre-emptive strike/regime change without an adequate intelligence bureaucracy to determine, *without doubt*, the intentions of the nation-state that it has targeted. As a result, this country is now caught up in a guerrilla war in Iraq against heavily armed, dedicated, *insurgent* nationalist groups focused on defending their religion, culture, economy and society against an aggressor. Our actions are being perceived by most of the world community as intrusive on national sovereignty. Furthermore, as this dilemma becomes more costly in resources and lives, the administration has not revealed any viable solution to exit this debacle. International terrorism, on the other hand, has taken a back seat on our list of priorities! But terrorism is the real enemy! This poorly conceived intervention in Iraq has sucked up our entire existing defense resources and has left our real enemy, the terrorists, free to regenerate to attack us and other countries again!

We can hardly permit this perception to persist. We are a nation that contains only 5% of the world's population but we consume over 40% of the finite natural resources. We come across to much of the international community as condescending and arrogant. In the '50's we were perceived by the third world as the ugly Americans. This administration has exacerbated that perception in the last four years so that this ugly American moniker is held not only in the third world but also by nations of all levels. This administration seems to disregard this fact and relishes the position as the only superpower, as if this status protects us from 95% of the world. This is wrong! *If* we have superpower status, it is very tenuous indeed! For example, Russia, with its existing nuclear arsenal, could ally with any number of countries that we have infuriated with our arrogance and become far more powerful than we are. This could happen in a New York minute! China could easily become a superpower in the next few years. The Muslin world as an alliance could too, under certain circumstances. Keep in mind that China has WMD. Pakistan and India have WMD. And, of course, North Korea has WMD. There are dozens of other combinations of nations and alliances that our arrogance has alienated that could render this country impotent. We must work with all nations, at all times if we hope to survive in this current community of nation-states. The bravado of "with us or against us", "we will go it alone", "bring them on" and black/white decision-making belongs with the Dr. Laura's and the Rush Limbaugh's of the entertainment world. It is just not viable in twenty-first century international affairs!

Second, with John Ashcroft the administration has eroded the freedoms of the American people here at home with the poorly conceived and constructed Patriot's Act. Under the guise of protection against terrorists, the Justice Department has trashed some of our personal freedoms that we have enjoyed for over two hundred years. The purpose was to give the authorities the legal tools to ferret out the terrorists in our midst. However, while the act provides these tools to the policing authorities, it has exposed the loyal citizenry to the abuses of a police state. This cannot be tolerated in a country of freedom. Furthermore, while the administration focuses on restricting the freedoms of the loyal citizenry, the borders of this country are being left unprotected and hundreds, even thousands, of illegal aliens are crossing to the United States each day. Any number of these people could be terrorists bent on destroying this country from within. Our Border Patrol is still grossly understaffed and under supplied with proper equipment. The United States' border is a sieve! These people crossing our borders, at will, could easily bring the necessary materials into the country that could cause catastrophic damage.

Any first year graduate student in international affairs has spent numerous hours researching, discussing or debating the dangers of WMD materials exchanged on the international black market and the risk this activity poses to the United States with its weak border defenses. The scenario is that a stateless terrorist organization can clandestinely smuggle a WMD into the United States and detonate it causing huge damage in life and property. But because the stateless terrorists have no country, the United States has no retaliatory target.[1] This administration is intent on spending $80-$200 billion (that we don't have, I might add because of the huge tax cuts that went to the wealthy, Texas energy cartel and the defense industry, specifically Halliburton) on a missile defense system that technologically is unsound. Test after test of this system has failed! Besides, what country would attack with a billion-dollar long-range nuclear missile that could be easily traced back to the source of launch by the United States' existing intelligence satellite technology when the car/truck delivery bomb that costs a mere few hundred dollars has an efficacy of 100%?

Our nation-state enemies are not stupid. They know our satellite capabilities and they know that our retaliatory forces with seven, eight or even nine thousand nuclear warheads could rain on their heads if they tried to attack with a nuclear missile. Our nation-state enemies are not suicidal! True an *effective* missile defense system would be nice to have, but it must be *effective* and we have to pay the price! On the other hand, al Qaeda is well aware of the efficacy and economy of the clandestine car/truck bomb. (Our homegrown terrorist, Timothy McVey made that abundantly clear in Oklahoma City! Also, the car/truck bomb is the weapon of choice in the streets of Baghdad, Jerusalem, Tel Aviv, Gaza, the West Bank, etc.) The bottom line is that this administration has squandered the people's security with tax cuts for the wealthy and ineffective defense systems. It has funneled excessive funds to the defense industry for weapons that will not address the intrinsic defense issues of this decade and the next. The country is now at risk and the lives of our youth are in jeopardy because our

---

[1] I spent many hours discussing this scenario in seminar in graduate school in 1968! Ten years ago Tom Clancy wrote the book, *The Sum of All Fears*, covering this exact scenario.

leadership has not had the vision to use the surplus funds that were handed to them in 2001 to secure our safety. The leadership continues to spend money (now to be borrowed from our children and grandchildren) to meet today's crises such as the ill-conceived war in Iraq and on a foreign policy of preemptive strike/regime change. This is not right!

Third, on the domestic front this administration proposed a policy to improve public education with the "No child left behind" Act. A principal feature is to make teachers and administrators accountable. This is a good thing. The problem is that this principal feature is based on the faulty model of the Houston School system. The Houston model has been proven a fraud in the last few weeks. Furthermore, the accountability testing process has sucked valuable teaching time away from the classroom. No provision has been made to increase the classroom time of the teachers so that they can teach *and* test. The result is that the teachers have become frustrated and stressed with the new protocols. In my local community, teachers are leaving the profession at a time when we need them to stay and we even need to hire more. Testing in itself is not a panacea to the problem. "High test scores do not a scholar make." The youth of this country need intense, disciplined learning environments, free of the distractions of unruly individual children that consume an instructor's time and distract from the learning of the vast majority of the students. Books, computers and other learning materials must be supplied in abundance. No teacher should have to spend money from their meager pay to supply necessary materials to the classroom! And the buildings must be adequate, clean and attractive. (I substituted at the top high school in the city a few years ago and I was appalled at the state of disrepair of the facilities, particularly the restrooms.) This country should have the best facilities, the best teachers, the best equipment and the best materials in the world for our youth. This administration gives only lip service to this issue and the tax breaks go to the wealthy.

Fourth, this administration, particularly President Bush, has proposed an amendment to the United States' Constitution to deny equal civil rights to a designated minority by proposing the marriage amendment. For two-hundred years this document has been the greatest instrument in the history of the world to guarantee equal protection and freedom to a citizenry. As the population has matured over the years and has become more tolerant to diversity, the Constitution has been amended to accommodate this newly perceived tolerance. Discrimination against minorities has gradually fallen away from the American culture. Race, gender and national origins are no longer acceptable ostracisms of our communities. Sexual orientation cannot be discriminated against in the work place or in society in general. Now, this twenty-first century President with his narrowly focused fundamental Christian beliefs has decreed that a minority group with a different sexual orientation than the majority population should be denied equality under the law. This is not right!

Fifth, this administration has permitted personal religious beliefs to interfere with the sciences that will arguably change the basic health of the entire world. This short-sighted view of stem-cell research has stifled this country's standing in the intellectual and scientific world. Because the administration does not have faith in governmental controls to prevent excesses in stem-cell research, it proposes that all effective research in this genre be halted. This is not in the best interests of the citizenry.

Sixth, this administration has failed to resolve the issue of out of control medical costs to the citizenry. The United States ranks last in the list of industrialized countries regarding health care, healthcare costs and life expectancy. We are the richest country in the world by a large margin, but are dead last in this category! This is a government responsibility. I understand that this issue was inherited from previous administrations, but this administration is standing the watch now. Unlike previous administrations, this administration had the wherewithal financially from the huge surplus to address this issue. However, it chose to turn the money over to the wealthy who already can afford the best medical care in the world. Now there are 4,000,000 more of our citizens than in 2001 that cannot afford adequate health care. This is not in the best interests of our country.

Seventh, this administration has failed to address the issue of the insolvency of Social Security and Medicare. Once again, although the previous administration had not totally solved the problem, it had pointed the issue in the right direction with debt reduction and responsible spending only to have this administration divert the surplus to the wealthy few and increase spending to an irresponsible rate. This simply is not right!

Eighth, I do not agree with this administration's position on the pro-choice/pro-life issue. It is adamant on the repeal of Roe *v.* Wade. If one would read the details of the decision, I think that he/she could see many areas of compromise where the choice of the woman could be protected and the life of the viable fetus would be preserved.

Ninth, in 2001, after taking the election without the popular vote, President Bush identified himself and his administration as the administration of reconciliation and cooperation. Over the last four years the opposite has been the case. The schism of the congressional "aisle" has not been greater for decades, if ever. "You're either for me or against me" has been his operative slogan for the entire term. I cannot accept that this attitude is what the Founding Fathers had in mind when they designed a government of the People, by the People and for the People.

Tenth, this administration has continually advocated fewer taxes. They have successfully reduced taxes by $1.4 Trillion, to go mostly to the wealthy and the large corporations. But every sophomore business student knows that reduced revenues must be accompanied by reduced spending. This administration did only one-half of the fiscal exercise, the easy half! They have reduced taxes but have not reduced spending. In fact, spending has soared. Bureaucrats have been added to the government payroll in the interest of security. War has been "declared" and foreign countries have been invaded. This has not been responsible fiscal leadership! Over the period that we will reduce revenues by $1.4 trillion, spending on this administration's decisions will increase by $2.7 trillion or more. President Bush argues that he will not return to a "tax and spend" government. Well, I'm no macro-economist, but "tax and spend" is more responsible than "no tax and *more* spend".

The reasons that I have listed above are really only the tip of the iceberg regarding my concerns about the 43rd administration. I have not even mentioned the flaws that I see in the recent Corporate Tax Bill that the Republican dominated Congress has just passed. Even John McCain can't stomach such special interest feather bedding. The recent flu-vaccine supply shortage is another bureaucratic debacle that can be laid at this administration's doorstep. One would think that after four failures in five years to have adequate supplies on hand at the appropriate time someone in authority would correct the problem! Suffice to say, I cannot trust another four years of this country's future to this administration. I am definitely not going to contribute to the RNC that supports these policies. As I have asked in previous correspondence, please remove my name from your solicitation list. Of course, I know that judging from your previous performance, you won't bother.

Regards,

Thomas M. Bates
Cc: Los Angeles Times
    Washington Post
    New York Times
    Democratic National Committee

ON ATTACKS ON RIGHTS TO PRIVACY

Whoa! What is our leader doing to us now? Yesterday on the CNN Channel I heard that the president recorded another "signing statement" on a piece of legislation. Today I read about it in the newspaper. The new Postal Reform Act that came across his desk just *had* to be modified with one of this administration's tools to deprive the citizenry of another Constitutional Right. The new reform law reinforces the right to privacy in the handling of first class mail. It requires that a warrant be issued before a government agency is permitted to open a citizen's personal first class mail. This is not a new practice. In fact, it has been operative since the beginning of this Republic with, perhaps, the exception of the censure of military letters coming from the war zones in WW II. (But that censure fell under military regulations covering military personnel in war zones. The military always has had limitations placed on their Constitutional Rights while serving on federal active duty.)

The president penned in the comment to this Postal Reform Act regarding warrants: "in the manner consistent, to the maximum extent permissible, with the need to conduct searches in exigent circumstances." This "signing statement" to the Postal Reform Act applies to all American citizens! Are we all enemies of the State? Where does this paranoia end? For what price is safer?

I really have to struggle with this issue. First of all, I have some problem with the concept of the "signing statement". Apparently the "signing statement" has always been available to presidents because the article in the Riverside, California Press-Enterprise (January 5, 2007, page A-3) states that President Bush has availed himself to the practice for over 750 times during his presidency. The P-E goes on to say that this is more times than the aggregate of all of the previous 42 presidents. Even though I have read a lot of United States history over the last forty years, I have never run across the "signing statement" process that at first glance by a layperson provides for the President of the United States to alter any legislation to meet his Office's specific needs without any recourse by the congress. This is more dangerous than the veto power. In the veto the legislation goes back to the congress for further review and debate and then the veto can be over-ridden with a two-thirds majority vote. There is no apparent over-ride of the "signing-statement". The legislation becomes law with a convenient disclaimer that the Executive Branch doesn't have to obey if the president makes the arbitrary decision that it is not in his best interest. This can't be the design of the authors of the constitution! This president is using this process (apparently rarely used by previous administrations, even in times of much greater crisis than we find ourselves today) to consolidate power into a single branch of government! This is, in my opinion, a gross abuse of power!

This is not the first time that this administration has wrested the rights of the citizenry away under the guise of defending against terrorism. It wasn't too long ago that the administration announced that it reserved the right to investigate the book borrowings from this country's public libraries in the interest of public safety against terrorism. I thought the Constitution guaranteed such freedoms as speech and press. Hasn't the Supreme Court ruled that these freedoms include reading of the printed word regardless of the content? Furthermore, who in the administration has this authority and responsibility to monitor a citizen's reading list or their first class mail? How can we, as citizens, be assured that this person or agency in the administration does not have a personal vendetta against a citizen? Also, what persons are on this "watch list" that needs to be monitored? Are they really enemies of the state - or enemies of the administration? Are they democrats, or socialists, or libertarians? Are they Muslims? Are they atheists? How about Unitarians? Now, any United States citizen must be concerned not only about the type of literature that they read from a public library, but also the first class mail that they receive. Aren't all of these questions suggesting serious restrictions on the citizen's rights and privacy?

I am a United States citizen. I served honorably in the service of this country for nearly 28 years (over six years in the regular service and twenty-one years in the active reserves.) When President Bush and Vice-President Cheney were seeking political privileges to avoid going to Vietnam, I volunteered. I went to Vietnam, flew 87 combat missions (nearly 700 combat flying hours), and left my family to fend for them selves only to find out that the war was a mistake! I came home to be reviled as a killer of innocents. I resigned from the regular service (with over 1700 total flying hours in my assigned aircraft) to try to put my life together but I continued to serve for the next 21 years in the active reserves and never missed a training period or never missed my annual flight physical. I logged over 3000 hours in the reserves in my assigned aircraft that included eight combat missions. And I worked a full time civilian job during the entire 21 years. I really take exception to the idea that after this devotion to my country that two privileged persons, who wouldn't serve, are empowered to have my mail opened and read or to have my reading material monitored in the interest of "national security"!

George W. Bush didn't go to Vietnam. He couldn't even find the time to take his annual flight physical and he logged a mere 278 rated hours in his assigned aircraft (F-102) during his brief stint in the National Guard. All of his other flying hours were either in training at government expense (240 hours) or in a non-combat aircraft (a T-33 trainer for 55.5 hours, 9 hours of which were performed in the backseat) just to meet his required minimum flying requirements for pay purposes. The active Air Force often provides obsolete trainers to senior careerists who have been assigned staff duties but must maintain some minimum flying proficiency so that they can transfer back to the cockpit after their staff assignment is completed. These extra aircraft were not and are not meant to be used to provide opportunity for young and privileged lieutenants to circumvent their sworn commitments. George Bush went non-current in his assigned aircraft and failed to take his annual flight physical which was another severe disregard for his responsibilities. Lt. Joe Ordinary would have met a flight evaluation board, would have been severely reprimanded, called to active duty for a minimum of two years and sent to Vietnam. This didn't happen to George Bush! His final two years were served at the very minimum level of participation (and there is some question as to the validity of the documentation) in the National Guard and not in the assignment for which the government paid to train him. And he didn't have any legitimate other job during this time! He was partying or volunteering in a political campaign, for goodness sake, for one of his father's friends.

Dick Cheney didn't go to Vietnam either. He was granted six deferments. I lived during those times. You can't tell me that any Joe Ordinary from the lower or middle class could get six deferments. Come on, how many turnip trucks are there? The vice-president stated publicly that he had more important things to do. What were they? Get married? Have children? Go to graduate school (after failing at Yale)? How many names are etched on those black granite slabs that represent young people who just wanted the same things for which the vice-president got six deferments? Incidentally regarding graduate school, at my university, if you didn't make your grades you were immediately classified 1A and drafted. You weren't given the chance to apply to graduate school. For the ordinary person, he or she wouldn't be granted acceptance to a graduate school after failing an undergraduate curriculum, unless, perhaps, there was some political pressure applied to the school. But this president and vice-president who didn't see fit to accept their country's call as young men have orchestrated a monumental nightmare in the Middle East that has killed and maimed thousands, including Americans, coalition participants and Iraqis and put hundreds of thousands of others in harm's way.

Yes, needless to say, I take serious exception to these two condescending, arrogant people and their subaltern stooges from the privileged class for limiting my freedoms, disrupting the world order with ill-conceived, perhaps stupid, strategies, causing thousands of deaths, destroying thousands of families' wellbeing and spending trillions of dollars that are borrowed from future generations. They are, in my opinion, negating the Great American Experiment for their own selfish ends.

Regards,

ON BUREAUCRACIES

Well, last week the president delivered his much anticipated speech outlining how his new and improved strategy was going to fix the Iraq War. So much for creativity! More of our troops are going into harm's way. I cannot believe the lack of thought that is coming out of our federal government. The American people spend more on intelligence and defense than any other country in the world; perhaps, as much as ten times more. (The CIA has an annual unclassified budget of $44 billion. The budgets for the other fourteen intelligence agencies and the classified "black projects" are not available.) But these agencies can't come up with a solution to the Iraqi mess that has been created by this administration? Someone should be fired! No, perhaps we need to fire a lot of people! Our bureaucracies are just not doing an effective job. Of course, their response is that they don't have enough people to do the job, so they need more help. I don't think so. I've been there. One of my colleagues in government often joked that our greatest challenge in public work was how to cram ten minutes of work into an eight-hour day. Sure that was an exaggeration, but it contained a lot of truth. The solution is not to hire more people to do the work but to hire, train and manage competent, efficient people and give them the proper tools to do the work. The government should heed some of its own marketing slogans, "we're looking for a *few good* people".

Jack Welsh the icon CEO of General Electric for many years and, perhaps, the most effective business leader in America during that time insisted that in a profit motivated operation management should purge/replace the lowest performing ten percent of the work force periodically, while the top performers in the force enjoy rewards for their efforts by sharing in bonuses based on bottom-line results. This was not something new. It's a concept as old as organizational management. It's simply applying the carrot *and* the stick. Welsh's reasoning was that every organization had at least ten percent of the workers who were not contributing sufficiently to be retained. With each purge, theoretically, the workforce would continue to improve. Those employees in the workforce who were considered adequate during one year may fall to the low rung of the performance scale over the next several years, and find themselves purged from the organization. From my thirty years of experience in corporate management I think that Mr. Walsh was not far off target. The ten percent was not locked in concrete every year, of course. Management may only identify five percent one year or fifteen percent the next year. Certainly, if the organization missed its goals significantly, the staff responsible must be held accountable. I often marveled at the manager whose department had failed during the fiscal year and insisted that all of his people were outstanding perform-ers. Boy, now there's a head in the sand! But it would happen time and time again. Mr. Welsh dealt with this dilemma. We have to keep in mind, however, that he was always associated with profit incentive organizations. There was a measurable bottom line to readily indicate success or failure, effectiveness or ineffectiveness. Unfortunately, gov-ernment managers do not have the luxury of an identifiable "bottom line" score because government agencies are not profit centers.

In federal bureaucracies there is no bottom line. The profit incen-tive is not there. Profit sharing bonuses are not operative. This makes performance appraisal a bit more complicated. The task of evaluation falls more to subjective elements of performance instead of objective elements of performance. This opens the way for politicking, cronyism and favoritism. As these subjective factors come into play, people get lazy, do less actual work on the task and concentrate on the politics of the organization. This activity, in their minds, protects their current position, provides sub-rosa opportunity to undermine the positions of their peers and to vie for promotion by self-promotion instead of technical competence.

On the other hand, the bureaucratic managers loathe firing anyone because of incompetence or subversive manipulations for two operative reasons. One, managers are fearful that a lost position in their depart-ment or agency will reduce the power of the department because de-partment size, based on personnel numbers, translates into importance in bureaucracies. Therefore, a reduction in personnel signals a loss of organizational power. Or two, the managers are fearful the terminated employee might have, or actually does have, political pull at another level of the organization that would pressure the managers to rescind the termination at great embarrassment. As a result of these processes, coupled with the requirement under federal and state labor laws or department policy that involuntary terminations require provable, written justification, unproductive or incompetent employees are left on the job. (So many managers are not courageous enough or competent enough to complete *and* make available to the accused employee a written good-cause document for involuntary termination. My thirty years of management experience observed this to be the case over and over and over again). As a result of these conditions, bureaucracies evolve into political empires and they grow bigger and bigger, cost more and more, but accomplish less and less. The general public sees this activity going on at the local, state and federal levels of bureaucratic management. (It also happens in private industry as well, but to a lesser extent because of the profit motive.) The final result is that many government agencies are heavily overstaffed and grossly under-worked.

There is another factor that requires mention in this discussion. When faced with a mandatory cut-back in staff, either in the public or private sectors, the first thing that the typical manager will do is to cut the most junior and the lowest paid in the group. After all, the senior people have the most experience and even if paid more, that experience will make up for their increased pay. Is this really true? In bureaucracies the skill sets of the seniors have migrated from the technical skills for doing the tasks to the political skills to hold on to the job, undermine a peer or self-promote. In a word or two, the mission of the organization becomes secondary for the experienced. Survival, deceit and self-promotion are the primary motivators. So the junior technical workers who are focused on the mission task are fired and the self-promoters are left to collect their pay and benefits. Now these bureaucrats are scared but instead of rolling up their sleeves and relearning the technical skills to get the job done they intensify their political efforts. It is beneath their dignity and stature to do the "grunt" work anymore. Therefore, bureaucratic agencies are not only incompetent and unproductive but also overpaid. The hard solution is to know who the competent employees are at all levels and terminate the incompetent employees at all of these levels. This will keep the organization lean but efficient; and provide opportunity for the junior, productive employees with a viable and fair career path.

The military is a federal bureaucracy and suffers the same weaknesses in management effectiveness as its civilian associates. All of the services are awash in politics, cronyism, nepotism and favoritism. The effectiveness reporting systems for the officer corps' are a horrendous joke. Promotion is more a result of form rather than substance. "Eye wash résumés", "filling the squares" and "who you know" are far more important for the promotion cycle. The military would become far more effective if more field grade officers and generals were reduced from the organizations and more riflemen/women and junior officers were recruited, properly trained and supervised.

So from the discussion above, we can't place all of the blame on the president, I wouldn't think. *Or can we?* Is the president being given accurate information and prudent analyses from these agencies that are mediocre at best? Is he ignoring recommendations due to a lack of trust in the competence of these agencies? Or is he an arrogant elitist spinning information for his personal ends?

Regards,

ON BUSH RHETORIC

Yesterday, I read in the newspaper that the pentagon and the CIA have been tapping the bank records and the credit records of United States citizens without any approval from the courts. These two federal organizations have always been restricted from spying on citizens of this country. That is, until this administration took office. And the vice-president crawled out of his spider-hole long enough to sneer an affirmation that this was acceptable in light of the terrorist threat that exists. If this government activity continues in this manner it will become more and more difficult to determine, *"who are the terrorists?"* This president and his klatch of advisers continue to perpetuate *their* notion that: *"you are either with us or against us!"* In my mind this is dangerous to the American people and to our democratic processes. This administration seems determined to quiet all dissent; to reject prudent suggestion and squelch the will of the people. What kind of governance is that? Well, in my mind it's more despotism than democracy.

Today, I read that the administration has abandoned the practice of wire-taping United States citizens without a warrant who they suspect of communicating with foreign terrorists. This comes after many months of steadfast rhetoric that the executive office does not need a warrant for these wire-taps under the provisions of the Patriot Act. Did anyone in the administration even suggest that they were wrong or had abused the power of the office? Not on your life they didn't. However, now that the congress is controlled by the democrats, the electorate has sent a very explicit mandate opposing the war and this "other party" has the power of supoena; Bush and Cheney have simply backed away from the issue. In my opinion, I don't believe they have really stopped these shady, abusive practices. After living with the record of deceit of this presidency for six years I am very suspicious that this announcement is just another ruse to mislead the electorate.

I have read in the news that over the weekend over two hundred innocents have been killed in Iraq and twenty-seven of our troops have lost their lives in this nightmare. The slaughter continues day in and day out.

The president delivered his State of the Union speech Tuesday night. He begins talking about cooperation across the aisle. He offered that six years ago and then stuck it to the left side. During his administration that historic schism has never been greater. Does anyone think that things are going to change even with the balance shift to the left? I don't think so. Vice-President Cheney immediately took the hard line on the war as early as Wednesday morning. On Friday the president proclaimed "I make the decisions on Iraq!" The administration will continue to talk cooperation out of one side of its collective mouth and continue to follow its own course with its brains (what little there seems to be) and actions. The Democratic Party and its allied Independents must keep the pressure on. They now have the hammer in the House and, with some convincing of sensible Republicans, can have it in the Senate.

The president started his address Tuesday evening with an introduction recognizing the historic event of our first Madam Speaker. That was nice. Then he launched into his speech proposing a balanced budget in the near future and a retirement of the national debt in the foreseeable future. Did I hear that right? Am I to be impressed with that? Six years ago we handed to these people a world in relative peace, a strong economy and a current year surplus of $270 billion and a forecast to retire the national debt of $6 trillion (leftover mostly from the Reagan/G. H. W. Bush administrations) by 2006 or thereabouts. President Bush and his gang reduced taxes in 2001 $1.4 trillion (I got a check for $600 unwanted borrowed dollars that I had to pay back the next April 15th.) Other Joe Ordinary's got the same or less. The total amount received by 90% of the country's population constituted 20% of the tax cut. On the other hand, the Ritchie Elitists, who made up 10% of the population, got a whopping 80% of the tax cut! Since that time George W. has invaded two sovereign countries (Afghanistan, I admit was necessary) for "regime change". The legitimate battle in Afghanistan was executed well at first, but the mission was deserted unfinished to concentrate on the disastrous invasion of Iraq. I will speak to the Iraq blunder in other essays. Suffice to say for this comment that due to the tax cut (that 60% of the people opposed in the first place, by the way) this administration squandered the surplus and overspent the budget by several hundred billion dollars for each of the last five years. The deficit spending continues, in spite of the president's comment on Tuesday, and the national debt has increased 50% over the last five years to $9 trillion! What kind of responsible management is this! I would think that the professors at Harvard Business School would be appalled and ashamed.

Regards,

ON THE SURGE

Opposition to the proposed escalation of 21,500 more troops is increasing in intensity. The Democrats are nearly unanimous and more and more moderate Republicans are signing on for the fight. The statistics are out that over 34,000 innocents have been killed in the last twelve months. Add this figure to the estimated 30,000 to 50,000 innocents killed in the previous years (this is a very conservative number) and we have a pretty significant level of carnage. These figures do not include the innocents maimed or the US troops killed and wounded (over 3000 dead and over 22,000 maimed). If the ratio of US dead to US wounded holds true for the innocent population, there are, arguably, over 615,000 non-combatants (women, children, and elderly) who have received physical scaring in this war. This is a tragedy. There are other statistics that need to be broadcast to effectively challenge this administration's position on the war in Iraq. Over a million of the highest educated Iraqis have fled the country. There are over four million Iraqis who have been displaced from their homes. Think about some of these statistics in the context of a country that has only 25 million for a total population! The state of Texas has about 25 million people. What would that state look like if 600,000 were maimed, over 100,000 dead, one million of the best educated moved to other states and 4 million displaced from their homes? The physical and mental pain is unfathomable.

Let's spend a few moments on this current escalation in the Iraq War. The president is sending 21,500 more troops to augment the existing 132,000 troops already there. Our forces are required over the next six to eight months to embed in the Iraqi units to strengthen the Iraqi Army's resolve to bring peace to the country. This is coming from the mouth of the president who said in 2004 (just before the election) that the Iraqi government had 175,000 troops armed, trained and ready to fight for their freedoms and by the end of 2005 there would be a total 260,000 Iraqi troops armed and trained to carry the war to the insurgents. Where are *these* troops that are supposed to be doing the fighting and dying? Let me tell you. They DO NOT EX-IST! And they never did.

After the 2004 election the media ran stories that there really weren't 175,000 Iraqis armed, trained and ready to take their place beside our troops; there was, perhaps, one battalion (about 800-1000 soldiers) that our commanders thought could be trusted in combat beside our men and women. What was that 175,000 number all about? "Weeeell," the administration had a list of Iraqi men who were believed to be, maybe favorable to serving, *if* certain conditions were met *and* it wasn't *too* dangerous. Our young people didn't have those options before they were sent into the grinder. Could these Iraqis be mustered to sign up for a real firefight? "Weeeell," Some maybe/might/sort-a' would, show up.

Iraqi army forces got their collective noses bloodied in the battle near Najaf over the weekend. The first reports disclosed that we sent in some minor air support to help out. Now the real story is coming to light. Not only were some copter gun ships engaged but also F-16's and British fighter-bombers attacked with heavy ordinance. The Iraqi ground troops were completely pinned-down and about to be overwhelmed when the supposedly "elite" Iraqi Scorpion Brigade *and* the American 4th Brigade Combat team, 25th Infantry Division came to the rescue. Does this action by an Iraqi combat unit sound like a well trained and equipped fighting force? First of all, the unit was committed to combat with extremely faulty intelligence regarding this militia force. The mass and firepower of the enemy was completely underestimated. We almost had another Little Big Horn scenario to write about in the history books. To add salt to the festering wound, this militia force, "Soldiers of Heaven" are Shiite. How many of the Shiites in the Iraqi army are willing and anxious to go-over to the militia if the fighting really becomes critical and the US forces weren't near by to reinforce-in-mass? How many of our troops would have been lost if American support had already been diffused into the Iraqi army instead of the homogeneous 4th Brigade stepping into the battle?

The media is full of suggestions that the Iraqi Government Army is not loyal to the central "democratic" government of Iraq or the United States. There is considerable concern that our embedded troops will be turned upon by the Iraqi forces. Essentially the Iraqis cannot be trusted. What protection would our embedded soldiers have when diffused into and surrounded by a heavily-armed, overwhelming hostile force. I think that the term "fragging" will take on a whole new meaning! The president's plan not only will be putting our young soldiers *in* harm's way, but also "*embedding*" them in harm's way.

The president is starting to rattle his saber even more vigorously toward Iran in spite of his comments about solving his issues with that country by diplomacy. I can see where this is going! He says we will respond to conventional military aggression, but at the same time continue to negotiate through diplomatic means to resolve the nuclear issues! I can see the turnip trucks coming this way again.

Keep up the pressure.

Regards,

ON HIGH RANK MUDDLING

More discouraging news was in the paper today. The headlines read, "**War strategy takes beating,**" lawmakers from both parties and experts challenge Bush's troop increase.... Admiral William Fallon was quoted as saying, "What we have been doing is not working." "We have got to be doing...something different." Now *there's* some real guidance coming from the president's nominee to take over General Abizaid's job at US Central Command. Hopefully he spoke with more substance that was not reported in the news media. Help me understand why the administration has nominated a navy admiral to oversee a land war? Has the army run out of generals? I don't think so. Could it be that the best qualified flag officer in Middle East culture and politics in all of our services, General Abizaid, failed to win in Iraq? Did his criticisms of the administration's policies sound defeatist? Shush, is he one of those "against us"? Or could it be that Abizaid recognized the futility of the Bush War?

Buried on the ninth page of the local paper was a story from Sharon Theimer of the Associated Press stating that "hundreds of US troops in Iraq and Afghanistan have experienced shortages of key protective equipment including armored vehicles, road-side bomb countermeasures and communications gear...." How can this be happening in the best equipped military from the richest country this world has ever known? The discovery comes from the Defense Department's own Inspector General's Office. This is really disturbing to Joe Ordinary. Only yesterday, I read that 70% of the casualties are due to road-side IED's. This war has been going for nearly four years and we still haven't provided our young men and women with the best equipment. If we didn't have the right equipment when the war started, why haven't we invented, produced and distributed it in the last four years?

Molly Ivins passed this month. We sure are going to miss her.

The headlines are talking more about war with Iran. We've got to have our heads examined if we let this happen. With the record of deceit that this administration has perpetrated on the American people we are going headlong into another debacle. I don't know where the president gets the idea that we can even handle another front. Our forces are already stretched to the breaking point in Iraq. There are no trained forces left in the CONUS to send to the Iranian front. Most important I don't trust that we are getting the whole story anyway. At this point in this country's Middle East foreign policy caution must be the operative word.

An open conflict with Iran would have serious repercussions in Iraq due to the close ties of the Shiah majority in Iraq to the Iranians. It would not be unreasonable that the Iraqi government would dissolve under the pressures in such a scenario. With that situation, the Iraqi Government army would disintegrate. The United States would have its entire force of 150,000 troops scattered throughout a country in complete chaos. The US units would be in danger of defeat-in-detail. The president is sending another carrier strike force to the Persian Golf to confront this issue. (Is this force the 21,500 troops that he said he was sending? I don't think so!) What in the world can one carrier do to contain this situation? The carrier has about 80 aircraft onboard, but only a little over half are strike aircraft. Launching a strike with that size force is only going to piss-off a whole lot of Iranians. Or possibly, the force is going to strike the alleged nuclear facilities. The targeting would be a product of our illustrious intelligence community. After the smoke clears, Al-Jazeera and CNN would report that we hit two hospitals and three orphanages. The sad thing is that CNN will be correct and the United States would have a lot of explaining to do.

On the local front in this global war, our National Guard troops that were sent to help secure our southern border with Mexico ran into a touchy situation last week. It seems that a gang of Mexican outlaws confronted the soldiers. These hoods were armed with automatics weapons. The Guardsmen had to retreat because their rule of engagement required that they could only return fire in self-defense. In addition, the soldiers did not have the authority to take people into custody. The outlaws got away. What are we doing? What kind of security is this? We could have had a blood bath on the border and our troops would have probably taken the brunt of the affair. If the Guardsmen cannot detain people who are penetrating our borders at will, what good does it do to put them in harm's way? If we don't want Guardsmen to have arrest authority then every military unit should have a Border Patrol officer "embedded" with it to accomplish the task. I don't see where Posse Comitatus is an issue if the offenders are foreign nationals. We have to start getting serious about these problems that we are facing in the 21st Century.

All of our borders are at grave risk of penetration. We have known this for years and we specifically focused on it since 9/11. What has been done? Virtually nothing! President Bush created another bureaucracy and placed an Arabian horse aficionado as the head of it. Then he threw the Coast Guard, the INS and FEMA together and called it Homeland Security. After the disaster of Katrina the organization proved less than worthless, but expensive. This new bureaucracy couldn't handle a natural disaster. The NYPD and FDNY did a much better job on 9/11 with much fewer resources and less expense than this convoluted mess of an organization. Far more effective, I think, would be to have another branch of the defense department. One could call it the Homeland Defense Service (HDS). The mission would be for this organization to protect/defend all of the borders and ports of the United States and its possessions. Incorporate the Coast Guard, the Border Patrol of the INS, the Sky Marshall Service, Anti-ICBM units and perhaps, the DEA into this corps. (Have FEMA stand alone to concentrate on disaster recovery but with the authority to request National Guard support in significant disasters.) There may be other organizations that may have a synergy with this mission. If so, incorporate them into this HDS. Train these people as policing officers and paramilitary units with authority to arrest. Give them adequate equipment for the job and provide proper intelligence input. Have them properly armed and *supervised*! Of course, the current organizations, such as Coast Guard, Border Patrol SMS, and DEA would have to be expanded in manpower, retrained and *fully* funded.

We have to rethink the defense of our country in the 21st century. Funds need to be reallocated to support border defense and guerilla/

insurgency warfare. More now than at any time in our history we are faced with an enemy that can bring the battlefield to our soil. And it isn't going to come from ICBM's and manned strategic bombers. The threat is going to come in the form of highly-trained guerilla units with sophisticated WMD's strapped to their backs swimming across the Rio Grande or traipsing through the woods of Northern Minnesota, arriving in container freighters or landing on deserted beaches from pleasure yachts. If they don't have the WMD's on their persons, they will arrive with the knowledge to fabricate them from local materials once they're here. This country is vulnerable to attack and the more we divert our limited resources on obsolete, Cold-War defense systems, such as anti-missile missiles and air superiority aircraft, the more vulnerable we become. Our enemies know this, but of greater danger is the fact that they know we are not taking heed and finding remedy.

Regards,

ON REDIRECTING RESOURCES

I was hoping to spend the month of February coming up with some suggested solutions regarding the war, but the problems keep coming and coming. In my last letter I ended with some comments about homeland security. Perhaps, that is a good place to start with my suggestions on how to divert resources for the protection of this country.

The increased funding for the Homeland Defense Service (HDS) could come from a reduction in the Air Force and Navy. These two services have lost some of their critical mission since the close of the Cold War, but they still have departments and units dedicated as if the Cold War was still active. Let me suggest some AF/Navy units and equipment that could be reduced or eliminated.

Send the B-1 Bomber to the bone-yard. It has never been an effective weapon system even for the nuclear mission of the Cold War. It looks very good on paper but it seems to be a real "hanger queen". Continue to reduce the Missile Command of the Air Force. Submarine launched ICBM's should be the main nuclear force for any residual Cold-War threat that still exists, in my opinion. Some thought could go into eliminating the B-2 also. This aircraft cost far too much to produce and it cost too much to maintain. However, it did see some action in the early Gulf War. Having it fly from Missouri to the Middle East doesn't make any sense. And the sensitive nature of its skin that requires it to be housed in a special hanger seems a little silly to me. Here we have a combat aircraft that cost $2.25 billion each that can't stand the rain? The conflicts that have been primary for the last 20 years have been relatively low intensity/ regional affairs. Most likely this will be the combat scenario for the next 30 years. We don't need highly sophisticated weapons systems with very complex defense penetration technology for low intensity guerilla warfare. If we need a long-range manned delivery system, we should design a relatively inexpensive flying platform loaded with fuel to loiter at a stand-off position and launch long-range ALCM's (Air Launched Cruise Missiles). Perhaps a modified C-17 cargo aircraft would fit the bill. The manufacturer could stretch the fuselage and add a launch bay for cruise missiles. Strategic technology funds should be directed to improved guidance and longer range of the unmanned cruise missiles that this flying platform would be carrying.

The venerable B-52 fits the needs of the 21st Century war scenario very well. Interestingly, it has been operational for over 50 years and has served as a strategic nuclear bomber as well as a tactical conventional bomber. It has served in the Cold War, the Vietnam War, and both Gulf Wars I and II. It has been reconfigured for every air to ground ordnance that the US Air Force has ever devised. Arguably, it is the best combat aircraft ever built. While the B-1 sits in its hanger in Texas and the B-2 is constantly being fussed over, the BUFF (the acronym given during the Vietnam era meaning "Big-Ugly-Fat-Fellow") goes anywhere at anytime to perform its assigned mission. It should be the established standard for all combat aircraft for serviceability, cost effectiveness, durability and flexibility. I think that it is safe to say the two aircraft to take the place of the B-52 (that cost less than $5 million/aircraft) have been very expensive failures. The B-1 cost 40 times more (at $200 million/aircraft) than the B-52 and the B-2 cost over **400 times** more (at $2 billion/aircraft) than the B-52!

Now, I will speak to the fighter aircraft that the US has in its Air Force and Navy inventories. This is much more complicated because there is such a diversity of weapon's systems in the inventories of the Air Force and Navy for tactical air warfare.

US FIGHTER AIRCRAFT

ACFT	ALT/SPD	CMT RAD	ARM	COST
Northrop Grumman (Navy) F-14	53/ft 1241mph	1239 mi	20-mm Ordn. 14,500lb	$25mil.
Boeing (AF)	60k/ft	1,222 mi	20-mm	

Aircraft	Altitude/Speed	Range	Armament	Cost
F-15A/B /C/D	1650mph		cannon Ordn. 16,000lb	$35mil.
Boeing (AF) F-15E	50k+/ft 1650mph	790 mi	20-mm cannon Ordn. 24,500lb	Est. $40mil.
Boeing (N) F/A-18A/B /C/D	45k+/ft 1190mph	460 mi	20-mm cannon Ordn. 15,500lb	Est. $35mil.
Boeing (N) F/A-18E/F	50k/ft 1.8 Mach	472 mi	20-mm cannon Ordn. 17,750lb	Est. $40mil.
Lockheed Martin (AF) F-16A/B	50k/ft 1320mph	340 mi	20-mm cannon Ordn. 15,200lb	Est. $20mil.
Lockheed Martin (AF) F-16C/D	50k/ft Mach 2+	923 mi	20-mm cannon Ordn. 15,591lb	Est. $20 mil.
Boeing (Marine) AV-8	unk/ft 662mph	103mi	25-mm cannon Ordn. 13,235lb	Est. $20 mil.
Lockheed Martin (AF) F-117	35k+/ft 646mph	691mi	Ordn. 5,000lb	Est. $50 mil.
Fairchild (AF) A-10	35k/ft 439mph	620 mi	30-mm cannon Ordn. 16,000lb	Est. $10 mil.
Lockheed Martin (AF) F-22*	921mph	unspecified	20-mm Ordn. unspec	Est. $180 mil.

* The F-22 Raptor was scheduled to enter the active inventory in 2005, but has been delayed due to technical difficulties and cost over-runs. That's not surprising, cost over-runs and late deliveries are SOP in the defense industry.

These are the main models of tactical aircraft assigned to the Air Force and the Navy. Some of them have unique capabilities such as the AV-8 that has STOVL capability or the F-117 that has stealth technology. The A-10 was built with off-the-shelf technology at much less cost than some of the other fighters. The story goes that it was so ugly that the regular Air Force didn't want it in the operational inventory so the generals turned it over to the Air National Guard. When the aircraft proved its worth in the Gulf War I, the generals took it back into the regular Air Force. The A-10 proved again in Gulf War II that it was a very effective weapons system and at a fraction of the cost of some of the "prettier" fighters that are much more expensive.

Most of our current fighters have been operational for a good number of years and there are some new models on the drawing board and even prototypes in the test phase. The cost to maintain and fly this great variety of aircraft must be staggering! All of the aircraft mentioned have different power plants and different armament configurations. Therefore, each type needs different training for the maintenance crews, different training for the flight crews and a huge inventory of different parts to service the different types of aircraft. This must change! The taxpaying citizenry must demand economy in arms manufacture. I'm not saying to buy the cheapest (meaning poor quality); I'm talking about economical management principles to take advantage of cost reductions due to mass production, consolidated training and simplified logistics.

Boeing has the X-32 (Joint Strike Fighter); Lockheed Martin has the X-35 (JSF). Hopefully the pentagon will pick one of the two to replace all of the various fighters that we now have operational. One basic aircraft slightly modified to accommodate the special requirements for Navy carrier operations or short-takeoff-and-vertical landing operations for the Marines would reduce the cost of the varied maintenance specialties, flight crew training and the huge inventory of different parts that is now required to keep our current inventory of various fighters flying. We have to keep in the back of our minds however, that

Robert McNamara tried to do this very thing in the 1960's with the F-111 during the Vietnam War. The military fiefdoms fought over the design and finally the Navy refused to buy any. The design issues were substantive regarding the swing-wing concept but it was eventually overcome. But by then the F-111 was relegated to a reconnaissance role for the Air Force in a stretched version and designated the FB-111. The cost to the taxpayers for the petty arrogance and bureaucratic empire building runs into hundreds of billions, if not trillions of dollars. This bureaucratic nonsense cannot continue!

The aircraft that have proved exceptionally effective in the current Iraqi/Afghanistan conflicts are the drones. The model most familiar to the general public is the Predator. There are both reconnaissance and attack capabilities of this slow-moving, low-altitude propeller-driven aircraft. There have been more than several incidences where the Predator has served our forces well both in the recon and attack roles. I understand that more advanced versions of this weapons system are in the development phase. The power-plants will be reciprocating engines and jet engines. All of these model drones are considerably less expensive than the manned fighters and bombers that are currently in the weapons inventories. This reduced cost is not to mean that they are cheap or of poor quality. For example, the fact that the aircraft does not need all of the equipment and armament to protect the aircrew and provide emergency escape equipment reduces the cost considerably. I understand that the controller (pilot) can operate the drone from his home base in CONUS so there would be savings in not having to deploy him/her to a forward base. The maintenance crew, of course, would have to deploy with the airframe. Another reduced cost to this type of weapons system is that the training for the controller (pilot) would be considerably less than training a person to fly a high-performance aircraft.

I have read in the newspaper that a Predator system that includes three airframes and the control systems cost about $10 million. This compares with $200 million/airframe for the aircraft scheduled to replace the aging fighter fleets of the Air Force and the Navy. For that cost differential the United States could have a swarm of Predators over enemy territory for the price of one F-22 (the new stealth fighter already in the pipeline for delivery to the Air Force), or the X-32/X-35

JSF (whichever is selected). If one of the Predator airframes is lost in combat, only that airframe has to be replaced at a cost substantially less than $10 million. Furthermore, the additional cost benefit of removing aircrew from high-risk combat environments is huge, when search and rescue expenses, medical benefits for injured aircrew or survivor benefits for the families of lost aircrew are eliminated from the cost equation! Getting back to high volume manufacturing for air weapons systems would reduce the cost/unit even further.

The Predator drones are also natural systems for deployment along our borders with the Home Defense Service. Again, I have read in the news that the Government has already deployed some of these systems along the US/Mexican border. That shows a spark of creative thinking. But three or six Predator airframes flying occasional recon sorties is not enough. Ample systems must be deployed to cover the border 100%, 24/7. Furthermore, creative communications protocols must be developed and implemented so that the "boots on the ground" can respond to the "eyes" of the drones in a timely manner.

This letter is taking too much time. I will write again soon with more comments, hopefully to stimulate creative solutions.

Work hard. The future of the Great American Experiment is at stake!

Regards,

MORE ON RESOURCE ALLOCATION

In my last letter I spent a lot of time talking about military aircraft and how expensive they are to fly and maintain. I didn't include helicopters or support aircraft such as aerial tankers, manned reconnaissance aircraft, transports and importantly, the command and control aircraft such as AWACS. These aircraft require a few words by them selves. Generally speaking, these aircraft have a greater value to the guerrilla/insurgency warfare order-of-battle than the high-performance fighters and bombers, except perhaps the A-10 and the AV-8 that are both low and slow interdiction aircraft. Supersonic speeds and stealth technology are simply not required on the guerrilla/insurgency battlefield. Helicopters fit the bill for counterinsurgency operations very well. However, they are very fragile machines vulnerable to ground-fire and can be brought down with relative ease. Therefore, instead of spending so much on stealth and supersonic speed technologies, perhaps the military should spend more on light-weight armament materials to better shield the copter crews and their cargos of soldiers going to the battlefield and the wounded being transported from the battlefield.

Many, if not most of the aerial tankers are modified airframes of other commercial or military transports. At first, the Air Force used WW II B-29 airframes with larger engines and designated them KB-50's for aerial refueling. Also the C-97 transport was converted to the air refueling mission with the modifications to designate the airframe the KC-97. These worked reasonably well until they were required to refuel jet-powered aircraft. When jet aircraft became the receivers, the reciprocating-powered tankers simply couldn't fly fast enough to keep up with their customers. At that time they were replaced with the KC-135 with the airframe of the commercial Boeing 707 airliner.

Since 1957 the KC-135 has been the backbone of aerial refueling. For additional refueling needs, the Air Force and the Navy have converted a number of different aircraft for the refueling mission. The KC-10, a modified DC-10 commercial airframe, entered the Air Force inventory in 1981. The Air Force and the Navy converted the C-130 to a tanker modification for special operations and the Navy converted a light carrier bomber for the carrier-based refueling mission. Well, you get the picture; the aerial refueling mission is serviced, in my opinion, with the best interests of the taxpayer in mind. The basic concept of converting existing airframes to the air refueling role has been extremely successful and has saved the taxpayer huge amounts of money. However, many of these tankers are aging with the rest of the military fleet and future administrations and congresses must stay on their toes to insure that the military-industrial complex doesn't bamboozle them into some exotic airframe that requires expensive design, development and testing when an off-the-shelf airframe will fill the requirement quite adequately.

The same argument holds true for the reconnaissance, transport and command and control missions. All can be served well with off-the-shelf airframes with a minimum of conversion modifications to the aircraft. (The reconnaissance mission will, of course, be augmented by the Predator drones and reconnaissance satellites.) All of the several services can use these aircraft and the replacement parts to keep them flying can be purchased in bulk. These bulk purchases will yield quantity discounts without jeopardizing high-quality. In fact, the actual quality of the parts may even go up due to the large, long and automated production lines that can be run instead of small specialty production runs for a relatively few specific parts.

A final note regarding the airframes mentioned above. Several of them can serve a variety of missions beyond the military applications. For example, the tankers can be converted to water tankers to work the annual forest fires that destroy tens of thousands of acres per year and threaten whole communities. This hazard is not going to go away in the near future with the global warming cycle that is now being experienced around the world. As this threat worsens we will need a much larger fleet of super water-tankers to combat these natural disasters. The large reconnaissance and AWACS aircraft can easily convert to a support role in border monitoring. They will be a very positive augmentation to the Predators that are already flying limited sorties along the Mexican/US border. (I will address border defense in a later essay and incorporate my ideas as to how we must develop an effective posture to make us more secure.)

There is no doubt that we need state-of-the-art aircraft to defend this country from aggression. But it is most important, in this era of finite resources, that we make *efficient* and *cost effective* aerospace weapons-systems that *really* meet the needs of the battlefield. It can be done with creative thinking, tight controls over the industrial-military complex, a rein on military arrogance and elitism and responsible oversight of pork-barrel and ear-marks graft. I don't think we have been doing a good job at this!

Work hard. A whole lot of Americans want to see some positive changes.

Regards

ON THE WALTER REED HOSPITAL DEBACLE

Is this an outrage, or what? How many of these "You're doing a heck-of-a-job, Brownie" scenarios do we, as citizens, have to endure before this administration stops bamboozling us and leaves the public scene in utter disgrace? On whom do we hang this recently revealed absolute atrocity at Walter Reed Army Hospital? For four years we have been sending our youth into a deadly grinder without the equipment necessary to protect them from some of the battlefield injuries. Our sanctimonious leaders, both political and military, have been declaring that we have the best equipped and best trained and best armed military in the entire world. But painfully the truth seeps out that our multi-multi billion dollar Army and Marines are getting their clocks cleaned against a raggedy-assed militia armed with vintage AK-47's, RPG's and homemade IED's. How can this happen? The icing on the cake is this latest exposé splashed all over the newspapers. These American kids, who heroically face death under arguably false pretenses and are atrociously injured, are sent to the squalor of a building 18 to nurse their wounds! How disgusting!

How deep does this mismanagement run in the military bureaucracy? Lieutenant General Kevin Kiley and Major General George Weightman were contrite before the congressional panel. They said they were sorry. *They said they were SORRY?* What have they been doing to earn their pay and the respect as general officers? **NOT MUCH!** These *guys* (They don't deserve to be addressed as general or even doctor) should be forced out of the service at a reduced rank (less than a flag rank) and lose their licenses to practice medicine. But these two scoundrels, I'm afraid, are only the tip of the iceberg. For example, where are the staff officers that, upon orders from Kiley and Weightman, should have inspected Building 18 and the other facilities that are now or shortly will be under scrutiny? And when they found even the slightest deficiency, they should have insisted that the deficiency be cleared immediately. These miscreants haven't surfaced yet. We must hunt them down and expose their incompetence to the families of our wounded soldiers and marines.

I can understand that a major general may not personally and/or routinely inspect outpatient housing, but someone should! Within the short time between the breaking of the story by the media and the convening of the congressional panel the evidence showed that more than one written complaint had been filed through proper channels ("filing through proper channels is a must in a bureaucracy, otherwise, regardless of the horror of the situation, the bureaucrats do not feel any compunction to make corrections") about the squalor at building 18. The evidence appears that more than once a complaint reached the desk of Kiley when he was commander of Walter Reed and at least one reached the desk of Weightman in the last six months since he took over that command position. Did they just wipe their behinds with these documents on their way to the officer's club?

Kiley was in command of the hospital from 2000 to 2004. He did nothing but cover-up. Weightman took command in August 2006. He did nothing but soft-shoe around the issue and then asked forgiveness when caught. Who was in charge between 2004 and August 2006? What are his excuses? Were there no complaints between 2004 and 2006? I don't think so. Mold doesn't grow, then miraculously disappear for two years then reappear; paint doesn't peel from the walls, and then repaints its self only to peel again on Weightman's watch, and holes don't get into the floors, get repaired without a work order only to reappear in August 2006. There must be a major general US Army doctor hiding in the weeds somewhere on active duty or in retirement who failed our wounded between 2004 and 2006. Let's find his sorry ass and fire him too. If he has retired let's call him back to active duty and then fire him at a reduced rank and make him pay back to the taxpayer the excess retirement pay he received as a major general. I'm not done, yet.

Now let's ask about the colonels, majors and captains; and let's ask questions about the sergeants all of whose jobs are closer to the problems than the generals who are taking the heat. Where are their senses of duty, responsibility, and decent human compassion? Why wasn't someone willing to ruffle some feathers and pound on some desks? This illustrates the weaknesses in bureaucratic management. There are a whole slew of bureaucratic yahoos that won't make waves even to assist or make more comfortable our wounded heroes. Few bureaucrats are willing to step to the plate to hit the ball for common decency. The excuse from these people, either military or civilian, is over work and under pay. They have to be kidding. Try getting someone to answer the phone in a bureaucrat's office after the scheduled quitting time of 4:30 pm. If anyone's there it's the cleaning crew. If you stop by a bureaucrat's office at 4:35 pm, the place is deserted. If you stop by at exactly 4:30 pm, you are in danger of being trampled to death by the human stampede to the parking lot. If anything, with this exposed incompetent track record in government the people are UNDER-worked and OVER-paid! I know. I've tried to go to government offices at or shortly after 4:30 pm. I've tried to make the phone calls too. As a matter of fact, I called the OMB just the other day, *before 4:30 pm EST,* to get a copy of the 2008 federal budget. After being redirected several times by the automatic answering system; I was passed to the desk of a real person. Her personal answering machine told me (you guessed it) that she was away from her desk and to leave a message and my phone number and she would call back to me. I did, but she didn't bother!

I think it is safe to say that these two generals need to be joined by a lot of other people at the lower ranks. This country can't afford to have these morally sterile individuals ministering to our brave soldiers.

Lt. General Kiley resigned/retired a few days ago, one step ahead of the "sheriff".

Regards,

ON ACCOUNTABILITY

In my last letter I talked about generals Kiley and Weightman and their military staffs and all of the failures regarding the proper care of our wounded that has recently been exposed by the media and the congressional panel. I suppose that the responsibilities lay where the "buck stops". The question was where was the "buck" supposed to stop? In my opinion, it should have stopped or "slowed *way* down" when it hit the desks of the sergeant, the captain, the major and the colonel. Apparently it didn't, and for the time being, these people are off-the-hook. (I wonder if they are sleeping well at night.) Of equal importance, and lurking in the shadows off-stage there is another culprit that needs to witness a moral sunrise in this revelation. This institutional rascal traipses around under the guise of "civilian contractor". It has been around the government a long time. It is sold to the naïve bureaucrats that civilian companies can complete contracts at less cost and with higher quality than government workers can complete these contracts, because as civilian contractors they enjoy the efficiencies related to private enterprise, profit motive and competition.

One of the "excuses" that the generals are giving to the investigating committees is that the housekeeping duties of the Walter Reed Hospital Outpatient facilities were contracted out to a civilian company. This is a disturbing revelation to me. This company signed a $120 million contract with the US Army to take care of these facilities. The work was not done! Aside from the fact that this seems like a lot of money for janitorial services, the outsourcing that this administration has instituted throughout the federal bureaucracies apparently is out of control! The administration argues that the free enterprise system is much more efficient than anything that can be handled by a bureaucracy. As a result civilian companies have taken over work in FEMA, the military, even in the intelligence community. Actually, outsourcing has been the darling management technique not only in the federal government but also state and local government and the large corporations. Generally speaking, outsourcing to smaller companies or offshore companies is less expensive to the host entities, if and that's a big *IF*, the host manages its contract properly and if the contractor is competent and efficient.

Now let's go back to the $120 million housekeeping contract at Walter Reed. Apparently the work was not being done, but you can bet your life that the contractor was collecting its money! Why was this happening? Well, let me guess that the host officials, i.e. probably at the sergeants', captains', majors' and colonels' levels, weren't doing their jobs making sure that the work was being done according to specifications. Or, the contractor was incapable of doing the job and didn't feel any motivation to do the job! Ah, do I smell a rat in the administration's outsourcing agenda? Could there be a chink in the armor of the great enterprise system by the way that the federal contracting protocol is being handled in such a way that effectively eliminates lower costs and higher efficiencies? The answer is a resounding *YES!* **IT'S CALLED NO-BID CONTRACTING!**

The company that has this very lucrative contract with Walter Reed Army Hospital is the very same company that received the ice delivery contract during this administration's Katrina debacle. This company had a no-bid contract then but couldn't find New Orleans on a road map. As a result the victims suffered as the ice melted on the side of the roads. Apparently this company had the Walter Reed Contract first and was screwing that job up for more than a year before they screwed up the ice contract. Didn't anyone raise a red flag regarding the efficacy of this contractor? Or, did someone try to raise a red flag, but they were immediately silenced by a swift transfer to the Iraqi war-zone or wherever? (You just don't screw with Dick Cheney and George Bush, or their buddies!) As the newspapers have printed, the CEO of this no-bid contractor is an ex-senior executive of Halliburton during the time that Vice-President Cheney was the CEO of Halliburton. The air around this episode is really starting to stink.

What is going on in this administration is that the "powers that be" have and are eliminating the cost effectiveness and efficiencies from outsourcing to private enterprise by letting no-bid contracts that are based on cost plus 10%. The no-bid contractor submits the only bid to the government at whatever cost the *contractor determines*. The government agrees with the cost estimate and adds 10% for profit. There are no systemic controls to limit this gouging process. If the contractor has an inside communication with the highest positions in government, such as the Office of the Vice-President or the Office of the President, the opportunity for windfall profits is above excellent because no one in the bureaucracy will question the executive offices regarding possible favoritism. But you can bet your life that favoritism is there in any administration, particularly the Bush Administration. However, the taxpayer who foots all of the expense does not enjoy the benefit of good old American capitalist efficiencies!

I'll be talking about Blackwater next and Bush's private army paid for by the American taxpayer.

Regards,

ON THE ATTORNEY GENERAL

Isn't this *something*! In the last essay I said that I was planning to take on Bush's contract mercenaries, i.e. Blackwater. Then I take a few days off from the news to see my grandsons and return to find that the Attorney General of the United States is about to be canned for incompetence or worse-a lack of integrity. Blackwater will have to wait until I get this current outrage off my chest. I agree with the senior Republican senator, who stated on the news media that if you can't trust the top law enforcement officer in the country to be truthful, then he should leave the office. Senator Chuck Hagel is also outraged by this latest development. I wonder why he doesn't bolt the Republican Party. He's seems against everything the Party stands for in this current administration, but then this administration is unique in that it has abandoned all of the traditional values of the Grand Old Party. Senator Hagel really has nowhere to go. His constituency wouldn't move with him. I think he is a true ally for the moderates on either side of the aisle. But even John Sununu (R.-N.H.), who, I have always felt, teetered on the precipice of the right end of the political spectrum, called for Mr. Gonzales to resign. Finally, this just was on "Meet the Press" on Sunday (April 1, 2007) and I don't think it was meant to be a joke. The news program reported that the "National Review Online" called for the US Attorney General to resign. If that bastion of American Conservatism can't stomach this administration's shenanigans, who can? There must be others on the right side of the traditional schism who are also outraged, but don't have the gumption to come forward.

There is nothing new about the president firing individuals in government who serve "at his pleasure". I understand it is done from time to time by both parties while occupying the White House. My conservative friends say "So what's the big deal? Clinton canned all of the appointed prosecutors in 1993." The answer is quite simple. The president has the authority to appoint people to jobs, but shouldn't dictate how they should do those jobs by holding job security over their heads particularly when the jobs in question have political overtones and the justice system is involved. In this current situation some of the Bush Administration's e-mails that flew back and forth during the planning stages of this "high-noon" massacre indicate that the administration requires loyalty to the Republican Party and the president at a disgustingly high level for job security, and that's putting it mildly! What boggles the mind is that this leadership is foolish enough to put such language in writing. Where have these people been since the dawn of the PC Age? Written e-mails just don't disappear into cyberspace.

Apparently, at least six of the eight prosecutors released by the Bush Administration were doing an above average job according to their performance reviews, and the other two were in the middle third regarding performance. What they did wrong was look into apparent misdeeds perpetrated by Republicans or people friendly to the vice-president or the president. They were not just on "fishing trips", but following legitimate leads into wrong-doing. Carol Lam, for example, pursued Representative Randy Cunningham all the way to the federal slammer. Some of the slime that she uncovered during that Herculean effort provided a slippery path to others friendly with the Bush Administration. She got canned for that? Something really stinks in the kitchen!

One head has already rolled for this debacle. Kyle Sampson had to fall on his sword early on in the attempt to thwart the Congress from asking too many questions. It didn't work   and, Mr. Sampson, who seems like an honorable man, testified under oath. During his testimony he refuted the Attorney General's statement that he (the Attorney General) wasn't involved in the discussions. At about the same time one of the top assistants in the Justice Department responded that she would exercise her rights under the Fifth Amendment of the United States Constitution if she were required to testify before the investigating committee. Finally, when the Congress suggested that Karl Rove and Harriet Miers testify, President Bush said that they would be willing to discuss the issue with an agreement that they would not be under oath, there would be no transcript and the discussions would be in private! I don't think that it makes much difference if Mr. Rove is under oath or not, because I'm not so sure if he knows the difference. So, with a shrug of the shoulders, the conservatives shriek that nothing is going on? Oops, Joe Ordinary *and* the "honorable" Congress are mighty close to falling from that darned turnip truck again, or so the White House thinks.

Tim Russert was interviewing Senator Hatch on his Sunday morning TV program, "Meet the Press", and, of course, the subject was about the Justice Department. At the end of this conversation that appeared to me to have Senator Hatch very much on the defensive trying to defend the Gonzales mob, Mr. Russert asked the senator directly if he would accept a nomination of Attorney General to replace Mr. Gonzales upon his resignation. I have never seen such a display of verbal soft-shoe in my fifty years of following domestic political science! It was just incredible! But then, how could we expect a very successful senator who is well regarded on both sides of the aisle to surrender his current position and, most likely a lifelong superb reputation, to take on a job that has been driven into the deepest possible political hole by an inept, no... grossly incompetent, lame-duck administration?

Keep up the good fight.

Regards,

ON BLACKWATER

Let's go back to Blackwater USA. For those who are interested, Blackwater USA is a billion dollar temporary employment company that supplies heavily armed "shooters" to the federal government for several activities in Iraq, such as VIP protection, convoy protection, sniper services (Is this a synonym for "assassins"?) and interrogation services. The company was founded by an ultra-conservative billionaire who inherited a fortune from his father then sold that company and started Blackwater USA in 1996. The company remained very small for the next five years, apparently catering to corporations that needed to protect some of their executives assigned to foreign countries that had unstable governments, until 9/11. There were some small federal government contracts during the Clinton Administration too, but they were relatively small in scope and did not pose any threat to the federal military structure. After 9/11 the United States Federal Government became a primary customer. This was very fertile ground for the defense contractors and specifically the civilian "shooter" companies because there was such a scramble to get friendly forces, of any ilk, into Afghanistan to confront al Qaeda and the Taliban. Congruent at this time of crisis, the new conservative administration was committed to outsourcing anything and everything that they could get their hands around including military weapons and personnel.

The day before the attack on the World Trade Center and the Pentagon, Donald Rumsfeld made a speech to his recently appointed Defense Department political stooges that his personal goal was to declare "war" on the stodgy military bureaucracy that he felt was endangering the security of the United States. The next day the Boeing 757's were crashed into their designated targets. The instant they hit the ground Mr. Rumsfeld had his nod to implement his design. Basically, his design included marrying smaller, Special Forces combat units to covert operations and supported by sophisticated weapons and "smart" munitions. In my opinion, this concept had real merit in this new century of warfare. However, this design was to be augmented by outsourcing military troop activities to private contractors. Also in my opinion, this piece of the ideological pie had some ominous undertones. Not only did this new military doctrine open the door for the private employment contractors to elbow into the cash now flowing from the Pentagon at an alarming rate but also, it opened the door to US Government financed "terror". This was the specific "lawlessness" that we were (and are currently) committed to alleviate in the Middle East and in other third world areas! The bottom line was that these contractors were not responsible to any authority accept the company's executives and, therefore, they were free to perpetrate atrocities on friendlies, enemies, or collateral civilians without accountability.

The greatest beneficiary of this new concept to employ civilian "shooters" was Blackwater USA that signed a "no-bid" contract with the US Department of State, and, perhaps, other "no-bids" with the CIA and the US Department of Defense, although other contractors participated in the cash grab on a more limited scale. (It is also interesting to note at this time that in the presidential campaign of 2000, the founder of Blackwater USA, Eric Prince, contributed substantially to the Bush/Cheney ticket.)

It is not difficult to surmise that a lawless shooter organization, contracted by the US Government and loosed on the international scene without control can wreak havoc on US Foreign Policy. This outlaw mentality among the civilian "shooters" has become rampant in the war zone that this administration has created in Iraq. In their drive to protect VIP's there is a no-holds barred protocol in driving innocent civilian Iraqis off the roads of the country or the streets of the cities. These innocent Iraqi civilians have their vehicles smashed if they happen to be in the way of a Blackwater-guarded convoy that is moving to or from US Government installations. If Iraqi civilians happen to be too close to a VIP caravan, *as determined by the Blackwater employees*, the civilians can expect to be fired upon by automatic weapons without warning. In the interrogation rooms the Blackwater interrogators are free to abuse, maim and even kill the detainees with no fear that they will be held accountable. In other incidents the Blackwater operatives have abused and denigrated the cultural and religious beliefs of the populace. If any innocent civilians or detainees are injured or killed by Blackwater employees, these employees, the company executives and the Blackwater Company are not held accountable for any of these lawless actions. This lack of control over this and similar organizations is an outrage! But that's not the whole story by any means.

The cost that the government is paying for this egregious activity is staggering. The no-bid contracts call for the federal government to pay as much as $950 per **"thug"**/per *day* for this service! For every man-year of "hired-gun" service billed by Blackwater USA the cost to the taxpayer is **$346,750**! It is estimated that Blackwater USA has over 2300 "shooters" working in Iraq and up to 20,000 more are available for service whenever the administration desires. In Iraq alone the cost to the taxpayer for this brigade of "rent-a-terrorist" equals (2300 X $346,750) **$797,525,000**! The cost of a brigade of US infantry for one year is approximately $134,900,000, which is only about one-sixth the cost of this "mob of thugs" whose behavior is tanking our good name with the rest of the world. Our troops are much better trained, disciplined and prepared to handle the issues of combat while adhering to the rules of engagement and the rules of law as well as the parameters of human decency than these "soldiers-of-fortune" who are employed by Blackwater USA.

There may be a place for hired civilian combat operatives in our military structure, but these people must be controlled. I have included a list of suggestions to accomplish this essential control for your perusal.

- All civilian combat operatives must come under the jurisdiction of the Federal Judicial system, the Uniform Code of Military Justice or a newly established "Uniform Code of Civilian Contractor Justice" while operating in combat zones and under a contract with the United States Government.
- Civilian combat operatives **cannot** be retained by the US Government with a no-bid contract.
- All civilian combat personnel contracts must be reviewed by the GAO for accuracy and cost containment before they are executed. A congressional oversight committee must be

established so that the American people are properly represented in this control process.

- Salaries paid to civilian combat operatives must be comparable to the salaries of the United States Military.
- Benefit packages including medical coverage, dependent medical coverage and survivor benefits must be comparable to those coverage's provided to the United States Military.
- All civilian combat operatives must be United States citizens or non-citizens with proper United States worker documentation.
- All civilian combat operatives must not be convicted felons from the United States or any other country.
- All civilian combat operatives must complete psychological testing to preclude any overtly aggressive psychopathic tendencies.
- All civilian combat operatives must take an oath of allegiance to support and defend the Constitution of the United States and to adhere to all rules and regulations of the responsible military command. All civilian combat operatives must submit to thorough background checks before they are permitted on the contractor's payroll.
- All civilian combat operatives must be indoctrinated in the culture and religion of the civilian population of the region where they will be operating for the United States Government.
- All civilian combat operatives will report to and be responsible to the United States Military command structure for the entire time that they are in the Theater of Operations.

The success of the United States in a guerrilla/terrorist war depends on our ability to win the hearts and minds of the indigenous population of the region. The United States learned this over thirty years ago in Vietnam, but failed to take heed. The United States should have learned this lesson in the Nineteenth Century during the Prairie Wars (1840-1890) with the Native-American Tribes of North America, but the US Army didn't learn then either. The US Military missed another opportunity to benefit from experience with guerrilla tactics in the Philippine Insurrection from 1899-1902. Although the Marine Corps compiled a field manual on the subject of guerrilla war tactics during the Philippine Insurrection, this valuable text languished unnoticed until the Vietnam War. Some field commanders used its concepts in Southeast Asia from 1961-1973, but it never received widespread recognition among the field commanders. After our loss in Vietnam the Marine Corps manual once again found its way to the back shelf of the War Colleges' libraries. The lessons learned were quickly forgotten and the important writings on this means of war by Mao Zedong, Ho Chi Minh and Che Guevara were ignored. The military-industrial complex went back to the comfortable and *profitable* conventional war scenarios of mass armies and navies, large ships, supersonic aircraft and main battle tanks. Although some of the military intellectuals tried to keep the guerrilla/terrorist strategies and tactics alive in the classrooms at the war colleges, this line of thinking never seemed to get past the schoolroom doors.

Now we are faced with a world wide guerrilla/terrorist war. Even though our Special Forces troops have substantial counter-insurgency training, as a total force our military still falls short in preparedness, training and proper equipment for this grim scenario that is playing itself out in the Middle East and Africa. In this situation the United States does not have the best military organization in the world. This administration is trying to overcome these weaknesses with privatization, but in doing so it is squandering the good name of this country in the process because it has not established the means to hold these "privateers" accountable. It is time to recognize the hubris that is ingrained in the American politico-military-capitalist psyche and creatively adjust to the realities of this Twenty-first Century threat.

The challenge is great in 2008!
Regards,

ON VIRGINIA TECH

I had to take some time off from my political thoughts to clear my head after the disastrous massacre at Virginia Tech. I only hope that the United States citizenry truly understands the price that is paid for the freedoms that we all enjoy. The tragedy at Virginia Tech illustrates how this price precipitates into our entire culture by the ugliest possible means every moment of every day. The pundits were immediate in their rhetoric that this episode would renew the debate over gun control and the people's rights under the Second Amendment. Fortunately this did not happen in the first hours of the tragedy before the families had a chance to put their loved ones to rest. Now that a few of weeks have passed, perhaps some thought can be given on this issue.

As luck would have it the United States Supreme Court has a case, District of Columbia v. Heller upon which they have agreed to review and issue an opinion. This opinion of D.C. v. Heller will have an impact on the Second Amendment. We will review this tragedy at a later date after we hear what the current conservative court opines on this matter of the right to keep and bear arms.

ON GUN CONTROL

A couple of weeks ago I wrote a very long letter regarding my thoughts of our Second Amendment rights and the price that we have to pay as a society to maintain these rights due, in large extent, to the ambiguity of the language of the revered amendment. In the final paragraphs I suggested that it was imperative that all Americans, particularly those at the several levels of government to put aside the selfishness of politics that is so apparent today in the legislatures and bureaucracies. I suggested that the NRA be given a chance to participate in open-minded discussion on the problems with the existing gun-laws that so infuriate the right-wing but fail in their endeavor to protect the general public from such tragedies as Virginia Tech and Columbine; and additionally, that the left-wingers "get real" in their overly protective stance for individual privacy at the expense of the public welfare. Actually, both philosophies are guaranteed by the our great United States Constitution, but the authors of that document left the rational and mutual accommodation of these rights to the intellectual maturity of posterity. *We are that posterity!* Although recently, my faith has faltered that as a citizenry we have abandoned our fiduciary responsibilities to these august authors of representative government, I now have some renewed hope that we can redeem ourselves. Last week on June 14, 2007, Flag Day, I was pleased to see that the House voted on a bill to clarify the existing gun-laws so that they can effectively save us from some of these on-going tragedies. The bill appears to be agreeable to the majority of the political spectrum. It still has a way to go before it becomes law but as long as it is not burdened with cumbersome amendments that would render it superfluous to reality, we may have something viable. Hooray!

Now, I am sure that this action by the House was not precipitated by my recent essay. According to my brother and confidant, my letter was much too long for anyone to read. (He should know, because he's an attorney and has to read many long convoluted treatises.) He suggested that I break it into two or possibly three Letters. I tried, but failed. I just couldn't see where I could cut it and maintain any continuity of my thoughts. I am sure that for anyone who tackled the letter in one sitting, happy hour would roll around much too soon for the task to be completed. Anyway, I feel that at the very least, that some of my thoughts are the thoughts of people in positions of power in this country. For this I feel gratified.

My conscience remains troubled from my work on the Second Amendment, however. As you may recall I wrote an essay that covered my thoughts on Blackwater USA and the mercenary business that this current administration has used so extensively in Iraq and paid for with tax dollars under no-bid contracts. In my mind there is a connection between the mercenary business and the Second Amendment that conjures up disturbing constitutional questions. What concerns me is the extensive use of corporate mercenaries and the rights and restrictions under the Second Amendment for the common citizen. The mercenaries are apparently under no restraints regarding the keeping and bearing of *automatic* weapons and large caliber weapons that *use explosive projectiles such as bazookas, RPG's etc.* The United States Supreme Court has ruled the prohibition of these weapons from the general citizenry. With this in mind the question is: where does the mercenary industry get the authority to possess and use these weapons in their execution of their business with the US government, state governments or private corporations for which they are employed? I don't recall any legislation exempting these private companies from the laws of the land. Furthermore, I am not aware of any variances to the decisions by the United States Supreme court or the interpretation of the High Court's adjudication regarding the limitations of the Second Amendment. Do these companies such as Blackwater, Vinnell and others have special privileges that the common citizen does not have? Did they receive these privileges by contributing to the political war chests of the Republican Party, or more specifically to the neo-conservative warmongers in this current administration? How far do these interpretations go? For example, can any incorporated business, such as a lawyer's private practice, or a chiropractor's practice or a general contractor, skirt the law of the land simply because they have filed for incorporation? I sure wouldn't think so! Someone needs to rein in all of this trampling of our most important legal document.

Work hard!
Respectfully,

Post Script:

Today, I read that Michael Bloomberg switched his party status to unaffiliated. There's a lot of dissatisfaction in the general population with both the Republicans and the Democrats. The electorate is really fed up with all the politicos appearing to be on the take in some manner or means. (I can't believe that Hillary didn't have more finesse when she was reported to be riding around in some company's corporate jet.) I don't think Bloomberg would be so gauche. Of course as we all know, he can buy his own jet and personally finance his own campaign, so this wouldn't be an issue with him. If he wanted participation from the electorate, he could ask for donations of only a dollar from individual citizens and tell the special interests to take a hike when they came for special favors from the government. The little guy thrashing around to make ends meet would be putting a lot of faith in one man's moral scruples, but that scenario has a refreshing ring to it after the last six years. As citizens we have to do better!

ON DOG DAYS OF SUMMER 2007

So, the calendar has turned another page and everyone should be back at the office by now. The only ones who seemed to keep a tight schedule over the last six or more weeks are the self-professed candidates for the presidency …um, plus one non-candidate, you know, the big guy that you see on TV on Monday, Tuesday, Wednesday, Thursday and Friday on the A&E channel. These folks were hard at work grinning and gripping around the country, mostly in the Midwest, all of them wanting desperately to be recognized by Joe and Jill Ordinary. The Congress, on the other hand, went home to hide from their constituencies hoping not to be recognized for their un-stellar performance for the first six or seven months of this term. I don't think we should be too harsh on them about their non-performance, after all, the Democrats do not have a slam-dunk majority to overcome the obstinacies of the White House and there is a twelve year backlog of mess to address, particularly the catastrophes of the last six years. The Iraqi Legislature also went on vacation in August (assuming that we call its non-work over the last couple of years something other than paid vacation). Furthermore, our president went to his ranch to chop wood and the vice, I suppose, remained in his spider-hole at the Naval Observatory. (Who can tell where Mr. Cheney ever is?) Anyway, not much productivity has come from these "august (?)" groups of world leaders during these dog-days of summer of 2007. I wonder, (it's just a *crazy* thought), if any of these folks truly harbored in their minds that during their leisure time some 80-120 American soldiers and Marines have been killed, another 450 have been maimed for life, another 600 wounded sufficiently to qualify for the Purple Heart; 2500 non-combatant Iraqi men, women and children have been killed, an unknown number maimed and another 100,000 Iraqi's have lost their homes and are refugees in their own country. It seems to be a minor subscript to mention that another 9-12 billion US dollars has been thrown into this black hole of folly during this August "vacation". I hope everyone has had a good time!

But as we all know, the hot summer has been productive for the Democrats. Karl Rove has finally left the White House. Now we only have to keep track of that fellow so that he doesn't stir up more trouble for the rational people of the country. Some of the talking-heads say that he will attach himself to one of the candidates running for office. I wonder who it will be. Are Rove's politics too conservative for Giuliani? I think so. But Thompson may be the man. I don't think Thompson is as conservative that he wants the Republicans to think that he is, but Rove seems to be a better fit there. He may stay behind the scenes so we best keep our eyes open. In my mind Mr. Rove is, perhaps, the most dangerous person in this country regarding the drive to relieve the Ordinary's of their civil liberties. Although Mr. Rove has been discredited in his tactics of late, he still holds strong influence over the ultra-right.

Alberto Gonzales threw in the towel during this last month. I think we all will heave a sigh of relief when he actually vacates his office at Justice. The man has done exceptionally well in pulling himself from poverty and discrimination but he was totally unfit for the rigors of the Washington scene. His presentation before the Congressional committee was shameful. His unfettered loyalty to the president and his apparent deference to the rich and well-born have done a great disservice to the general public and his cultural heritage. As one of the media pundits commented, just what constitution did he study at Harvard?

As the heat wave abates in this southern California region that I call home, I wait without much hope for the Petraeus Report. This administration is "dripping water" on the direction that it will take regardless of the Report and regardless of the negative findings of the GAO, or any other audit. We will stay, in strength, for an indefinite time! Perhaps a small percentage of troops may get to come home, but they will go immediately on the return list twelve months from now. The president is trying, and I fear he will be successful, to delay the hard decisions for the next administration. That's still seventeen months in the future! Surely as we live, the new administration, regardless of party, will not have a viable plan upon arrival to the White House. Furthermore, the Congress will still need to bless it in some way; so corrective action will be several more months away. All the while another 1400-2000 or more of our soldiers will be killed, another 13,000-20,000 or more will be wounded, another 25,500-35,000 or more non-combatant men, women and children will be killed, and another $153-$207 billion or more will be spent. Our military will be exhausted and perhaps, dysfunctional against the **real** war on terror.

As I have always told my people in the business environment, don't come to the table with a complaint without your very best solution. Your best shot at a solution may not be the one that is used but it may be the catalyst that generates the best solution. Intelligence identifies problems; genius solves problems! And more often than not, genius comes from more than one brain. I'm afraid that the only solution to the Iraq venture that is going to come down the pike is not going to be a pretty one. I certainly have my ideas about this whole issue regarding our security, i.e. war on terror, border security, military might and competence, internal security, immigration, etc. However, I don't have the space in this letter to put them down in writing, so I'll do it next week after I hear what General Petraeus has to say. In the meantime we complain about the cost in lives, in money and in National goodwill of this folly, but I don't think that we really can imagine the cost in these three areas that will be required to implement viable solutions.

Respectfully,

ON THE IRAQ WAR

I am waiting for the broadcast of General Petraeus' Report to the Congress and the Administration regarding his recommendations for the war in Iraq. By now most of the substance of his recommendations have already been leaked to the media and reported to the public, so I don't anticipate any surprises. We will stay, in force, for the foreseeable future. The carrot to the American public is that the military will revisit a withdraw option next summer. In the meantime, the casualties will continue for our forces and the Iraqi civilian population. In addition, no meaningful focus will accrue on the Afghanistan/Pakistan border where the real threat seems to be. So, as I mentioned in my last letter, I will present my thoughts on this debacle that we must address if we hope ever to repair the tarnished image of the United States on the international scene and hopefully limit any attacks on our homeland.

First of all, I want to address the Iraq War and what we, as citizens, must resign ourselves in the next five and a half years. (This includes the remaining months of this Administration and the next presidential term.)

1. The **financial burden** is going to balloon beyond any of the current estimates. The last that I heard was $600 billion spent to date and another $400 billion of unidentified expenses that have accrued but not reserved. In my opinion, this aggregate of $1 trillion will be only half the total cost, perhaps even less than half the total cost, considering the losses to corruption within our government, the corruption in the Iraqi government and the incompetence of the federal bureaucratic management (including the military). For example:

- The need to lease Russian transports to move the MRAP vehicles to the Middle East is going to be hugely expensive. The

Russians have us over the barrel in negotiations for this lease because of the immediate need to get this equipment to the war zone as quickly as possible and the fact that the Russians are the only game around with the big transports. This dilemma is the result of military procurement screwing around for three years before the vehicles could come off the assembly line in quantity. If military procurement was competent, the vehicles would have been available much sooner and transported to Iraq by ship and already saving some lives.

- The manpower requirements for a continued reliance on a voluntary military force will require that the mercenary vendors continue in the combat area at a cost far above that of comparable military forces.

- The loss of small arms weapons that are distributed to Iraqi militia who have intrinsic loyalty to our adversaries has already cost millions and will increase dramatically as our forces increase reliance on these people.

- The cost to support our physically disabled veterans will increase arithmetically with each new wounded soldier. Survivor benefits costs to families increase with each soldier's death. (I won't even attempt to address the social losses to the families and their communities.)

- Military equipment losses will cost billions to replace. We have already fallen far behind in the replacement of equipment that has been lost to this unnecessary war. We have to re-equip quickly in order that we remain a viable power in the world as we move beyond this historic debacle.

- Every Iraqi structure that we have destroyed and will destroy until we end this conflict will have to be replaced. This includes infrastructure, industry, homes, schools, hospitals etc. This cost alone will cost hundreds of billions of dollars, even if we do it efficiently; without the scourge of corruption. (Now that's a fantasy thought!)

"**Hey!** Enough of this rehash of the costs. Where are the solutions? Where are the sources of the money?" The solutions are not pretty, but I must stop at this point because to add the next segments will make this letter too long.

I'll be back in the next couple of days with the financials or "Where is the money?"

Respectfully,

Post Script: General Petraeus presented his report this week and *Newsweek* ran their article on the general's "brainiac brigade". After nearly five years, the Administration may have finally found some people who have intrinsic knowledge on what they are doing; and can recognize opportunities in an insurgency environment. I'll address this more in tactics and strategies. In the meantime, we shouldn't negate positive action by partisan bickering and posturing.

TMB

ON COMBAT SECURITY CONTRACTORS

"Back-fill" units play a critical part in tactics and strategy in counter-insurgency areas of operations (AO). However, I understand that the current military structure does not have the resources and manpower to support these back-fill operations now or even in the immediate future. Furthermore, the unpopularity of the war in Iraq precludes us from employing some of our allied militaries with these necessary skills to cover these activities. Civilian civil engineering, economists, building contractors, natural resources specialists, humanitarian organizations, etc[2] may be deployed in lieu of military specialists in this environment but careful consideration must be made as to how these non-combatant civilian organizations are protected. This security requirement for civilian contractors can be handled by several different means.

- **US Army/US Marine Corps** military police units. These people are specifically trained and equipped to handle static defense lines around stationary locations. These units performed these tasks commendably during the Vietnam War. Also, these people have been trained in how to deal with the civilian host nation population just like some of the better trained highway patrol agencies and local police forces in the United States. The current problem in Iraq is that there are far too few companies of these specialists in either of the services, because the manning document for these units have been purged to supply increased manning for the infantry units. Military police units in this role

---

[2] See Army FM 3-24 (University of Chicago Press: Chicago) 2007, pages 60-65.

cannot be supplemented by line infantry or artillery personnel because these traditional combat soldiers have not been trained in the delicate nuances of civilian personnel management under stressful conditions. If Army FM 3-24 is followed in this Iraq War and reconstruction of the host nation's infrastructure is to take place simultaneously with the suppression of the armed insurgents, a substantial requirement for highly skilled security police must be deployed throughout the country. The Army and Marines should address the increased manning of the military police MOS.

- **Civilian Security Contractors**. At the present time and since the beginning of the Iraq War the Bush administration has used civilian security contractors to provide protection for visiting VIPs to the AO and to provide protection for civilian contractors both non-government contractors/organizations and government organizations. Most notable and perhaps, most infamous, is Blackwater USA. I have already spoken at length about Blackwater USA in previous essay and raised serious concerns about the efficacy of "for-profit" security contractors operating in a counter-insurgency environment. Since September 16th, Blackwater USA has splashed over the front pages of the media for their alleged massacre of 17 unarmed Iraqi civilians in an unprovoked shootout in a Baghdad intersection. Per usual a congressional hearing was called and Blackwater USA founder and CEO, Eric Prince was called before the group to explain his company's position on the matter. All of this took place before proper investigations were completed. Neither side had substantiating evidence regarding this incident. The end result was some scolding from both parties and from what I could gather from the media, the committee members were short of the facts (because the independent investigations were not complete) and Mr. Prince defended his company's position with the aplomb of a founder and CEO. Mr. Prince was contrite and welcomed oversight from the appropriate agencies (that have been lacking since the beginning of the war) of his operations but steadfastly held to his position that Blackwater USA honored the requirements of its federal contracts in that no person under Blackwater security had ever been injured nor anyone killed. In my mind Mr. Prince won this confrontation on points, but the essence of the matter; the intrinsic concern of the incident at Nisoor Square was not addressed.

As pointed out in every text ever written regarding success in counter-insurgency/guerrilla warfare, the *safety* and *confidence* of the indigenous population **must be secured!**[3] The massacre at Nisoor Square by an American contractor in the employ of the US State Department is arguably the most counterproductive action that could be perpetrated on the Iraqi people and their alleged sovereign government that is struggling to survive the travails of this war. The US State Department came forward with assurances that a full investigation would be conducted and any wrong doing would be addressed. Within a day State representatives interrogated a witness, Ahmed Abdul-Timan, for three hours trying to intimidate him to change critical specifics of his story so as to vindicate the Blackwater personnel from any wrongdoing. Fortunately, the State Department failed in this outrageous malfeasance. But the damage is done! The United States has shot itself in the foot one more time.

Should Blackwater take all of the blame? I don't think so. Blackwater USA is satisfying the conditions of its contract with the United States Department of State. It has delivered at 100%! Their clients in their care have never been killed or injured. The tactics they use to maintain this superior record or the aggressive behavior of the Blackwater employees both on and off duty has not been challenged by military authority or the IG of the State Department or the Justice Department over the several years of Blackwater contracts in the AO. The Nisoor Square incident is not the first questionable action by Blackwater over the last several years. Last December a drunken Blackwater employee killed an unarmed friendly, an employee of the al-Maliki administration in the Green Zone. This perpetrator's only punishment was that he was sent out of the country and allegedly fired. That action lasted only six

---

[3] See Army FM 3-24, pages xxv, 65.

months, however. Within this six month period this person was back in Iraq working for one of the other civilian security companies. Over the time span of the last year, other evidence has percolated out of Iraq that Blackwater has killed at least 21 other Iraqis and wounded at least 27 others in at least six other violent incidents.

Blackwater and the other civilian security companies were exempted from Iraqi jurisdiction by Paul Bremer in Order 17 issued two days before he left the AO and *after* Iraq was granted sovereignty. And Mr. Prince and the other CEOs of the other security contractors know this. How can Bremer's Order 17 stand? Are al-Maliki and his government only puppets for the Bush and Cheney administration? Does the new Iraqi government have no sovereignty? Apparently not, since up to now Order 17 has been operable. **It is time to change!** These contractors **MUST** be held accountable!

Today's news reads that the State Department and the Iraqi government are negotiating the withdrawal of Blackwater from the AO within six months. This will probably cost the taxpayer another billion dollars or so because the Blackwater contract is being cancelled without Blackwater violating any contractual covenants. The Associated Press article goes on to say that sources from State and the security community suggest that the Blackwater employees and other assets of Blackwater in Iraq will be taken over by one of the other security contractors in the country. If this happens without careful review, this is a recipe for an ongoing problem! Why? Let me explain.

Eric Prince, who is an ex-Navy SEAL, and his staff have very carefully recruited Blackwater's employees from the military with special attention given to those who have experienced combat and especially those who have Special Operations training with combat experience in the Middle East. Many are ex-Navy SEALS or from other Special Operations units. On the surface this seems to be a good formula for recruiting people who will work in a dangerous combat zone guarding VIPs and diplomatists. Even the VIPs and diplomatists have vocalized their preference for Blackwater protection over military police because of Blackwater's efficacy. But herein is the rub. These specially trained soldiers hired by Blackwater typically operated in "free-fire zones"[4] while in combat. According to psychologist Dave Grossman, a former army Ranger, and author of the definitive book, *On Killing*, the people that have been selected by Blackwater for security missions, such as ex-Navy SEALS, ex-Marine LRRP[5] members, ex-Army Green Berets and ex-combat experienced veterans, a high percentage of them, in all probability, have a low resistance to killing. Although highly decorated, loyal to their company and country, brave, even self-sacrificing, these men have been conditioned to kill, have experienced killing and are predisposed to kill in a violent environment.[6] Hence evolves Blackwater's reputation of a company of "cowboys", "Rambos", "trigger-happy", "shoot first/ask questions later", "hired guns" or "US sanctioned terrorists". Therefore, before these people are permitted to continue security work in the Iraq counter-insurgency AO under another name or company, they must be screened for excessive, aggressive tendencies and reoriented toward a higher resistance to kill. In addition, all security contractors must come under jurisdiction of the Department of Justice, the DOD/UCMJ, and monitored by the IG of the Department of State. Army FM 3-24 and all other counter-insurgency literature are **emphatic** that the indigenous population be made to feel confident of their safety even at higher risk to the counter-insurgent forces, including visiting VIPs and diplomatists. This can't happen unless proper measures and oversight are taken to reorient and continually monitor the activities of the civilian security contractors.

We'll continue this discussion in my next essay.

Work hard. There is a very long row to hoe before we get out of this mess.

Respectfully,

---

[4] A Free-fire zone is a designated area where all indigenous people are considered the enemy and armed and dangerous. This includes women, children and the elderly. The Special Operations Forces, while operating in these locations have authority to kill anyone in these designated areas that even hint to be a threat to the mission or could expose the SOF's position to the enemy. Free-fire zones are normally located in enemy controlled areas.

[5] Long Range Reconnaissance Patrol

[6] Dave Grossman, *On Killing*, (University of Chicago Press: Chicago), 1996, pages 177-185.

ON INDIGENOUS SECURITY FORCES

Indigenous Iraqi Police Forces. Continuing my dialog regarding security forces in the Iraqi AO, the final group, and in my opinion the best choice in a counter-insurgency environment (not to be confused with the most efficacious choice), are the indigenous Iraqi police forces. This decision will probably cause much greater danger to the diplomatists and VIP visits to the AO. I can only say, reservedly, so be it. The Army FM 3-24 is very clear that the passing of security responsibilities to the sovereign authorities is paramount if the United States and the al-Maliki government have any hope to establish lasting control over the country. The greater dangers to the visiting VIPs and diplomatists are a price that has to be paid. And in my opinion, it is a legitimate price. Why do I say this?

- Well, first of all from what I can gather from the news media there are far too many self-promoters from congress and non-essential government agencies going into the AO in the first place. Also, if some of these people absolutely have to be in-country, I feel that they can get all of their information inside the Green Zone from real-time videos. These interlopers should be shuttled from the airport to and from the Green Zone by high flying helicopters at altitudes safe from small arms and with electronic-counter measures equipment. They should spend the shortest amount of time possible in the country. *And they should be there **only** for legitimate reasons!* The idea of congressmen and senators strolling through a market place with 200 armed guards and wearing a flack jacket and other body armor and after five minutes of presence declaring that the neighborhood is safe is just simply ridiculous! There is no self-respecting terrorist in the world that would even attempt to interfere with that idiocy being splashed over the media for the entire planet to enjoy.

- Second, the diplomatists, ambassadors, intelligence officers and other people are professional government executives who, in my opinion, have signed up to take the same risks for the defense of the Unites States as the men and women in the armed forces. This being the case if these people have to venture out of the Green Zone they go with full body armor and indigenous Iraqi police protection, as Army FM 3-24 highly recommends and as the Iraqi government deems necessary. The very idea that our State Department has missed the significance of indigenous police security and opted for a civilian contract security force that is not tightly controlled, to execute protection for State in a reckless modus operandi that kills unarmed, indigenous innocents while working in a counter-insurgency environment, is so counter-productive that it is *beyond* appalling.

- Third, the indigenous Iraqi police forces have not received a very high mark in the way of competence. This increases the risk to those the police are supposed to protect and it is just one more very good reason for the non-essential VIPs to stay away. However, the bigger issue is; why haven't the Iraqi police forces fared better in our evaluation of their competence? As I look at my notes from 2004 when I was following the presidential campaign, I recorded that the Bush Administration just before Election Day insisted that somewhere in the neighborhood of 180,000 Iraqi troops and police officers were ready to take over the security responsibilities in-country. A week or so after the election the public was informed that the 180,000 figure was *slightly* in error. In fact, only one battalion of Iraqi troops was considered ready to take the field unassisted by US troops. One battalion is approximately 800 soldiers! Where did the other 179,200 soldiers and police officers go? It turns out that there weren't even that many names on rosters! We citizens were bamboozled! This happened three years ago. Even now, there are not nearly 180,000 troops and police trained and ready to take the field independent of US troop supervision. Why not? The US Army and the US Marines can take an American youngster off the street and have him/her combat ready in six months to fight for someone else's freedom. Something squirrelly is going on if the Iraqis can't get their act together to train their ex-military and their ex-police to secure their own country in four years! Be that as it may, I think we are compelled at this point to put the Iraqi troops and police in charge of neighborhood security NOW!

This being the case, in my opinion, the tactical approach for the US command is to loosen the reins on the Iraqi security forces and let them sink or swim in the defense and security of their neighborhoods and their protection of supply convoys, visitors and diplomatists. The "coalition" forces should back off from the neighborhood operations and secure the Kurdish region and the borders between Iraq and Iran and Iraq and Syria. Then the US Government should place in escrow (or whatever the proper instrument is in international finance) a sum of $100-$200 billion (perhaps it may require more) to have available for the Iraqi's to use to rebuild their country once they resolve their religious/political issues between Shiah and Sunni factions. Of course, Iraq must be stable for any of this to work. Meanwhile, we should continue to support the tribal leader's movement away from support of the al-Qaeda miscreants that have invaded the country due to the political vacuum that we created. This will not be easy as tribes can and will turn on each other in this volatile environment. But we have to give it our very best shot! This will take very close management and sound judgment from the authorities that we assign as tribal liaisons. Also, our military forces, in addition to securing the borders as mentioned above, should be available to help the tribal militias to eliminate the al-Qaeda from the region.

Let's give this topic a rest for the time being. Blackwater USA is back in the news for allegedly screwing the US citizenry out of millions of dollars in taxes. Go get 'um Henry Waxman! We'll talk more on strategy next time. Incidentally, I am going on-line with a website in the next couple of weeks @ www.jusinbello.com if anyone is interested.

Keep up the good fight.

ON THE IRAQ WAR IS NOT *THE WAR!*

The War is the *Global War on Terror.* As we all know now, and the Bush Administration knew before the preemptive invasion the United States perpetrated upon the Iraqis in March 2003, the Iraq incursion was based on four criteria that really had little to do with the global war on terror. These criteria were:

1. Iraq's tyrannical dictator, Saddam Hussein, allegedly had weapons of mass destruction and was expected to use these weapons against Israel and the United States.
2. Saddam Hussein had murdered significant numbers of Iraqi citizens in the past and his brutal government was continuing to perpetrate these atrocities upon the Iraqi people.
3. Hussein attempted to assassinate President George H. W. Bush a decade earlier.
4. Saddam Hussein and his Ba'ath Party were harboring and giving other aid to al-Qaeda before and after 9/11.

First of all, there were no weapons of mass destruction in Iraq in 2001-2003. Any that had existed after the first Gulf War were discovered by UN inspectors and destroyed. All intelligence that alluded to existence of WMDs surviving the destruction was unverified and of dubious value. As it turned out the information suggesting that WMDs existed in 2001 was not true. Second, Hussein did execute significant numbers of citizens in the Northern provinces. This happened in the 1980s and was based on solid evidence that these citizens were attempting to overthrow the Hussein regime and assassinate Saddam. (There is also evidence that the United States intelligence community was aiding this clandestine scheme and similar schemes after the first Gulf War in 1991 involving the Shiah Muslins in the Southern part of the country.) The Middle East is a very harsh political environment and Saddam Hussein's brutal actions were probably in line with any other totalitarian dictator or monarch in the region. Third, there is evidence that Hussein ordered an assassination attempt on George H. W. Bush; there is also evidence that Hussein suspected that President Bush authorized the rebellions against the Hussein regime. Fourth, there was no hard intelligence that Saddam Hussein was harboring and aiding al-Qaeda before March 2003. In fact, the most reliable evidence indicated that Hussein was paranoid of the al-Qaeda; he was even fearful that they may execute a successful coup against his regime. Al-Qaeda established their cells in Iraq only after the invasion and the defeat of the Iraqi Army by the United States and only after the collapse of the Iraqi government infrastructures and the law enforcement agencies. In my opinion, nations do not perpetrate preemptive attacks using dubious intelligence. In order to be legitimate in the international nation-state system, a preemptive attack on another country must be based on rock solid intelligence of that country's imminent attack on the former.

Now that al-Qaeda has embedded in Iraq, I suppose there is reason to surmise that the Iraq War has become an adjunct to the Global War on Terror. However, compared to the rest of the world where al-Qaeda and other Jihadist extremists operate, Iraq is something less than THE WAR. The Iraq War is defined more appropriately as a battle, a theater of operations or area of operations. This being the case one must consider the cost in lives, treasury, resources and reputation to the United States to this effort. That cost has to be added to the 80,000-100,000 (perhaps hundreds of thousands more, depending on who is counting) innocents dead and the near total destruction of the Iraqi infrastructure. In war theory there is an old cliché that goes something like this; "You don't want to win the battle, but loose the war." There is also a great anecdote that came out of our failure in Vietnam that illustrates this concept. After that war, a group of United States military scholars joined in a seminar in Hanoi with some of the North Vietnamese senior officers who were our adversaries between 1961 and 1973. One of the US colonels asked one of these North Vietnamese officers the question that went something like this; "What do you make of the fact that in every firefight between our forces, the US soldiers or Marines prevailed every time?" The Vietnamese officer replied, "The fact may be true, but it is also irrelevant."

In Iraq we have spent $600 Billion, lost 3800 soldiers and Marines and have had over 30,000 wounded. Our active military and reserves have been stretched to the limit of human endurance by repeated rotations to the battle zone. The end is not in sight. We are loosing huge amounts of equipment and lives to the civil war aspects of this situation. Al-Qaeda and their allied terrorists can easily withdrawal after they have used Iraq to season their warriors to fight us somewhere else in the world. These Jihadists can easily take *THE WAR* to the United States because our borders are still so porous. All this while, we continue to have an exhausted military pinned down in Iraq.

The Bush administration insists that we have to stay in Iraq so that we don't have to fight the Jihadists in this country. I think just the opposite. I think that the Jihadists can come or withdrawal from the battle of Iraq with impunity and they will, when they are ready. But I don't think we can; and to me, that's very dangerous.

Respectfully,

ON FINANCIAL SOLUTIONS

I'm back again with my thoughts on solving the crisis this current administration has generated for us. As you recall in the last six and a half years we have **over** spent the federal budget by nearly $3 trillion. About $600 billion has gone to Bush's Iraq War, a conflict that was ill-conceived, poorly planned and totally unnecessary. It has exposed this country to the great dangers of Jihad or any other aggressive behaviors. However, we can't waste more effort pointing fingers at this humongous example of poor judgment. History will do that! Our job is to fix the problem. I'm afraid that it will take hundreds of lives, years of time and billions in treasury. So let's get on with it.

The **financial solutions** are buried in government systemic waste and incompetence. Listed below are some possible opportunities to reduce other federal expenses and divert the savings to the war effort:

- **The federal civil service** is grossly overstaffed and underworked. The greatest challenge in most, if not all, federal departments is "How to squeeze ten minutes of work into an eight hour day." Because of this lack of meaningful work by the bureaucracies, unnecessary busy work has been generated so that people can look busy and justify their existence. Bureaucratic fiefdoms are everywhere! This must change! The best and quickest way to do this is to reduce the work force. For most departments a 10% reduction should be mandatory. (I can guarantee that in an efficient private business environment these departments would operate at 50% fewer employees. It just takes some hard-nosed, competent management!) But 10% is a good start. For some departments 20%-30% reductions would be very reasonable. Good examples of a 30% reduced work force are the congressional staffs serving the "Do-little-other-than-posture" legislators that the American citizenry has suffered with during the last several years. (This comment is directed to Republicans **and** Democrats.) A 15% reduction overall of the government civilian work force and the expenses saved from the elimination of the superfluous busy work would release $4,500,000,000 per year to help pay for the war. (Formula: 450,000 employees X $100,000. Very conservatively, the 100K includes salary, benefits, expenses and the elimination of superfluous work.)

- The **federal subsidy programs** must be drastically reduced or totally eliminated. The milk/farm subsidy is a good example. Currently we have budgeted billions of dollars to the dairy farmers. These farmers all live in palatial estates and drive expensive cars. To think that they qualify for government subsidies until they reach a million dollar annual profit is appalling! I read just the other day that the farm subsidy being debated in the Congress now totals $286 billion. There are subsidies for corn, soy beans, wheat and God-knows-what-all. Most, if not all of these funds are going to profitable agribusinesses and/or well-to-do people. Why do we permit this to happen? Furthermore, there are government subsidies going to profitable businesses and industries as well. For example, the oil industry is sucking up federal funds when the oil companies are making enormous profits and rewarding their CEO's with huge salaries, millions of dollars in bonuses and outrageous perks. Another example is the weapons industries that are billing the government with ridiculous prices due to no-bid cost-plus-10% contracts. Why? The neo-security industry is charging the government 4-6 times the cost to deploy a security guard than the cost to train and deploy a US soldier or Marine. We have to cut this nonsense out **NOW**! Our efforts will save billions of dollars on an annual basis.

- After reading *Legacy of Ashes*, by Tim Weiner, I feel strongly that our **intelligence community** needs to be completely revamped, reorganized, substantially reduced in size and reduced in budget. This sounds counterproductive, but it became more evident yesterday (December 3, 2007) when our intelligence people reversed their analysis on the threat of nuclear weapons' development in Iran. Intelligence is our most important weapon against global guerrilla/insurgent/terrorist warfare, but it must be competent, accurate, and thorough! We can't afford half-truths and shoddy work being fed to an administration cocked to the preemptive strike mode. We spend far more than any other country on intelligence gathering and analysis. The incompetence displayed with the analysis work that got us into the Iraq War and the information fed to the administration regarding the Iranian threat is unconscionable. Over the last decade or two our emphasis has been on technological intelligence systems. These systems are important (read *Body of Secrets* by James Bamford), but currently, we need HUMINT (human intelligence) to deal with the Middle East situation. HUMINT can be less expensive than elint or comint and it is more applicable to the guerrilla/insurgency scenario. This change of focus to HUMINT could save billions. If the "black programs" could be analyzed for efficacy perhaps much more could be saved.

- The **Military** could contribute considerably by reducing or eliminating Cold War weaponry, the maintenance of this specialized weaponry and the manpower associated with the operations of this equipment.

Air force production of the F-22 could be cut and the down-sized contract extended over a greater number of years. We don't need an air superiority fighter at present. The advanced models of the F-16 and the F-18 still satisfy this need adequately. I don't know of any country in the world that has a fighter superior to these two. The media announced that China had a new high performance fighter, but it looks like a knock-off of the SU-30 to me. The F-35 production should be expedited, perhaps, because it has capabilities more in line with counter-guerrilla/insurgency operations. Eventually we can replace the F-16 and F-18 when the need arises, but not NOW! This procurement strategy could save another $40-$50 billion. The intercontinental bomber mission has been reduced since the end of the Cold War. Therefore, some if not all of the B-52's and the B-1's could be retired. The B-2 should be able to handle the diminished intercontinental strategic mission. The retirement of the B-52's and the B-1's;

their maintenance support, aircrew reductions, munitions support, base support, etc. would save another several billions of dollars over the next decade.

Navy could help save money by reducing its surface fleet. No other country in the world has multiple surface fleets at sea simultaneously. We should cut to a *reasonable* superiority from an *overwhelming* superiority. This would save billions of dollars. The submarine fleet may bring some minor savings, but this weapon system needs to stay intact because it will take up the slack from the retiring strategic bomber fleet mentioned above.

As a final note, however, we may have to expand the **Combat Marine Expeditionary Force** transports with associated helicopter and Harrier (or F-35) squadrons based on the decks. These units provide a rapid strike capability with a coordinated mix of combat force to respond to emerging crisis situations in the Third World. Perhaps, existing aircraft carriers could be converted for this expanded mission.

The savings from the above recommendations could easily amount to $50- $100 billion a year, perhaps more. If we need more funds, the alternative might be the dreaded; increase taxes/lay-off more employees/cancel more government contracts. Believe it or not, this country's treasury is finite!

Respectfully,

ON THE UNITED STATES ARMY

The armed services are the bureaucracies that we will discuss in the next several essays. We will also look at some non-traditional armed bureaucracies such as the Coast Guard, Border Patrol and Intelligence community-paramilitary operatives since they share an equal burden in the guerrilla/insurgency scenario.

The tactical and strategic solutions for the next ten to twenty years will focus on guerrilla/insurgency warfare. Therefore, the benefits of the savings in costs and manpower from the reductions discussed in my previous essay should be directed to the above agencies. Let's take them one at a time.

The US Army is woefully under-manned, under-trained, under-paid and under-motivated to successfully protect this country from the combat threats of transnational organizations and belligerent nation-states over the next two to three decades. The major inadequacy is that the US Army, as a whole, has been formally trained only to defend against conventional attacks that are perpetrated by nation-states. For the last forty or more years, counter-insurgency/counter-terror and guerrilla warfare has been relegated to the special operations unit (Green Berets, Navy Seals, and AF Special Ops, IC- paramilitaries and, perhaps, some specially trained Marines). All of these several units have been under-funded, understaffed and under-recognized since their inception. In many cases voluntary assignment to these organizations (and all members are volunteers due to the extraordinarily dangerous nature of the mission) was a career-ender to the officers and NCOs. With this in mind let me make a few suggestions.

The US Army tradition of specialization has to be modified. Let me be clear. All soldiers must be trained first as infantry before they specialize in artillery, engineering, armor, ordnance, intelligence, procurement, etc. ***AND*** all must stay proficient in the infantry skills and tactics. This will increase the training costs of the army, but guerrilla/insurgency warfare has no traditional front lines and everyone in the combat zone is vulnerable to attack. In fact, guerrilla/insurgents' primary targets are rear echelon facilities. By the very nature of their limited armaments (In Iraq our adversaries use primarily AK-47/74s, RPGs, IEDs-roadside and car bombs.) and small operational units, they cannot sustain a frontal assault against a well-armed and trained conventional army. Guerrillas seek out the weakest areas of their opponent such as logistics lines, command posts, supply depots and rest areas. The US Army does teach infantry tactics and skills to all recruits in basic training, but once the new soldier has gone to advanced specialty training he/she no longer trains in these important basic infantry skills. Furthermore, conventional warfare tactics and counter-insurgency tactics must be taught and practiced ***in parallel*** on an ongoing basis for all US Army personnel to meet the expanded challenges in today's combat operations. There is just no excuse thirty years after we were defeated in a twelve year guerrilla conflict in Vietnam, eighteen years after the end of the Cold War, thirteen years after Gulf War I and continued insurgency operations in the Balkans not to be prepared to fight **either** conventional wars or counter-insurgencies on a large scale. This failure in military training, in my opinion, is unconscionable!

This ongoing infantry training is important. First, it will reduce the need for civilian security contractors to guard the VIP and supply convoys, and some of the rear echelon positions. I might add that the security contractors can be reduced even more by keeping all of the non-essential, self-promoting legislators and bureaucrats out of the combat zone. These visits are very expensive to the taxpayer when we have to pay $600 a day for security guards to protect these people. These visits also disrupt the focus of the military leadership because the generals and colonels are obligated to brief them on the operations and the rank and file have to service their comfort needs.

Second, this infantry currency training of all army personnel will provide a larger pool of manpower to rotate into the combat patrol role. At present, army clerks, artillery cannoneers, supply people, mechanics, tank drivers, etc. are most often exempt from participating in the counter-insurgency roles. This leaves too much manpower on the "sidelines" of the real battle. When all of these specialists are subtracted from the total number of troops (169,000 with the surge additions) we have in the Iraq combat zone, fewer than half, at most, and probably closer to only 20% who actually pick up a rifle and move out to the battle. **This must Change!** "Boots on the ground" in guerrilla/counter-insurgency warfare means troops actually shooting at the enemy; not just some shooting while others fix trucks, tanks and helicopters or shuffle bureaucratic paperwork. Think about it! If 20% is a realistic number of coalition riflemen on patrol in Iraq and 20% of 169,000 equals 33,800, then we are actually at parity in combat strength to an enemy estimated at 35,000. All scholarship including Army FM 3-24 insists that to win we need a preponderance of combat forces of several fold.

The US Army must get more combat productivity out of each soldier, NCO and officer. Specifically I am referring to senior NCOs up to E-9 and field grade and general officers. This may sound crazy but a major general makes about one-third what a Blackwater USA/International civilian security guard makes in a year. To put senior NCOs and senior officers back with the troops would sharpen their wits and strengthen their physiques. I can recall my last days before retirement from the active reserves. When I went to a major military headquarters or to the Pentagon, I was appalled at all of the over-weight, physically unfit senior NCOs, colonels and generals huffing and puffing along the halls. It appeared to me that some of these active duty people were having trouble just getting up the stairs. This is not a comforting sight! This should not be. General Tommy Franks stayed in top shape when he was in charge, even with his rigorous schedule. General David Petraeus looks very fit too; as do some of the other officers in the field. War is a very physical activity even in this modern era and ***all warriors*** must be physically fit!

The US Army must increase in manpower. I think that the Air Force and the Navy are overstaffed at the present because both services maintain large inventories of Cold War weapons systems. If the Cold War units in these services were reduced in size, then the personnel assigned to them could be deemed supernumerary. A novel idea is to transfer this surplus manpower to positions in the US Army. There would be an initial retraining cost, of course, but the costs would not be as great as eliminating the individuals from the services with severance packages and starting from scratch with new recruits off the civilian streets. Some of the critical skills of these AF/Navy people, such as mechanics, electronics technicians, intelligence specialists and ordnance specialists could be transferred directly to the army mission. All of the transfers would bring with them the very important universal military mindset of discipline, deference, sacrifice and honor to country. The only training costs would be the infantry skills and tactics training that would be mandatory.

This transfer of manpower would increase the US army by as much as 100,000 and relieve the burden that is currently on the army divisions rotating to the combat zones. As a last resort, the draft has to be considered in this manning discussion. It is hard to swallow, but we are up to our ears in this mess in Iraq. It will take a substantial military to accomplish the tasks necessary to complete what has been started and repair the damage to the Iraqi people and our international image. In addition, even if we satisfy the manpower needs to extricate us from this unnecessary war in Iraq, we still have an ever growing crisis in Afghanistan and Pakistan that must be addressed NOW! On top of all of problems in the Middle East, we remain extremely vulnerable at other locations around the world and along our borders at home.

The US Army must change its pay structure to give a realistic incentive to the soldier to pick up a rifle and head out on patrol. The services already pay bonuses to pilots, doctors and some other specialists. Essentially these are high skill, but low risk positions. Bonuses are necessary for the high risk jobs too! The army should be paying a significant bonus to the combat soldier in the field, perhaps $100-$300 for each patrol that he/she completes. This bonus is in addition to the soldier's normal pay, allowances and specialty bonuses to which he/she is entitled. Let me be clear on this following caveat; **the rear echelon cadre should get *zip* of this combat bonus, unless they pick up a rifle, climb on a Humvee or MRAP and get in the real fight too.** This goes for the over-weight NCOs, mechanics, clerks and officers. This program would have to be monitored, because rear echelon people are prone to makeup frivolous patrol assignments for themselves around places such as "Green Zones" or other safe havens so that they can file for this special pay, but take little or no risk. That practice is pure nonsense!

ON THE UNITED STATES MARINES

In my last essay I concentrated on culture changes in the US Army so that the service could better confront Terror Warfare in the 21st Century. This piece will focus on my opinions of the United States Marine Corps and what changes, if any; need to be made.

Marine Corps combat culture is the model that the US Army should adopt. For as long as I can remember all Marines consider themselves infantry first and specialists second. Whether or not everyone in the Corps stays current with infantry skills and tactics, I can't say, but the mindset is a great start! In the Army once soldiers pin on the crossed cannon, crossed sabers or aviation wings, etc. they seldom return to retrain in basic skills and rarely think in terms of infantry. The nuance is small but as long as the tradition of being an infantryman first and always, as the Marines do, the psychological process to stay current in the skills and tactics of this most basic military endeavor is far easier. In my mind, current basic infantry skills are essential to a counter-insurgency force. The Marines must make sure that they follow through on this very important factor when assigned to counter-insurgency operations.

Marine Corps' boot camp training has always been considered more physically challenging than the Army's basic training and I am sure there are veteran soldiers and Marines that would support either side of this argument. The important end result is that both of these services must have all of their people in the best physical condition and at the highest level in combat skills because the troops will need to perform these skills under the most trying conditions. At the present time this is not happening, particularly in the Reserves and the National Guard units.

In the field the Marines are currently better prepared for the combat venues of counter-insurgencies than the army because of the emphasis on rifle skills, physical conditioning and small unit tactics. However, this service is also hamstrung with traditional conventional fighting doctrines that suck up training time and dollars. The Marines are trained on amphibious landings and conventional large unit tactics. The Corps has not had to charge a defended beach since Okinawa in 1945 or perhaps Inchon, in 1950. I suppose that we need some training in these techniques, but today most attacks on insurgency areas of operations, even from the sea, are undertaken by troops transported to the beach-head by helicopters. The heavy equipment such as tanks, Bradleys, MRAPs and artillery come after the beach is secured by the infantrymen.

Of course, this heavy equipment delivery to the beach hinges on the success of the navy clearing the approaches of sea mines, the very inexpensive but highly effective sea weapon of insurgent/guerrillas. The US Navy has ignored this very real threat for decades and is woefully deficient in mine clearing craft. This must be changed.

The manning of the Marines is too small for the counter-insurgency mission and like the US Army manpower must be given a much higher priority. This service could readily use the surplus personnel from the US Navy's obsolete Cold War weapons systems units.

Traditionally there has been an inter-service rivalry between the Army and the Marines. Most of it has been in good humor and many have deemed that it was harmless. It appeared harmless, that is, until the Granada invasion during the Reagan Administration. During that two-week "war" it became abundantly clear that all of the armed services, not just the Army and Marines, were not coordinating their combat doctrines with each other. This lack of mutual cooperation was the result of long years of inter-service rivalries mostly related to protecting the budget allotments that each service coveted so greatly. During the Granada invasion such critical information as communications frequencies were not shared among the services. The principle of "unity of command" fell apart. Who was in charge of the overall operation? Who was to support whom and when and by how much? The result was that the alleged "best" military in the world" (Actually it's by far just the most expensive military in the world; "best" is arguable!) fiddled and fumbled through a two-week campaign that required over 7,000 troops, multiple warships of various sizes, dozens of

fighters and helicopters to overcome a mere 267 poorly armed and totally untrained (in combat) *construction workers.* This cannot happen
in the 21st Century! When a terrorist leader sees this kind of botched
performance, *he sees opportunity.*

In the forward of the *Army Field Manual 3-24* there is great fanfare
that General Petraeus successfully orchestrated a joint effort between
his Army scholars and Marine General Mattis' Marine scholars to complete in record time a definitive doctrine and guide manual regarding counter-insurgency operations. This collaboration must evolve
into joint cooperation between these services in the field. This effort
identifies the need to comingle doctrines, tactics, weapons, equipment,
communication's frequencies and jargon if there is to be any hope at
success in a guerrilla/insurgency area of operations.

When the draft of FM 3-24 was posted on the Internet last year, it
took nearly two million hits. The book is now available in the book-
stores. In my opinion it is written in stilted "bureaucratese", but it
incorporates established counter-insurgency techniques in a refreshed
text and it should be read by all Americans who have an interest in
current military strategy. The manual, however, cautions that words
and doctrine do not make the changes in the cultures of the military
hierarchies. People do! Leaders do! Like all bureaucracies, armies
and navies are loathing to change. Herein lays a huge problem but
CHANGE MUST HAPPEN!

The organization structure of the combat division in both the US
Army and the US Marine Corps must be changed. As mentioned
above, the cannoneers and armored troops and all of the other specialists must be trained and brought to currency levels in small unit
rifleman skills and tactics. Organizationally, the combat divisions
must have significantly enlarged units of military police, civic affairs,
civil engineering, medics and transportation to operate effectively in a
counter-insurgency/guerrilla environment.

The transportation companies need enlargement so that civilian
contractors do not have to ride shotgun during convoy duty. Due to
loose controls, civilian contractors are detrimental to the overall operation because of errors in judgment by these people during tense
encounters with the enemy. In addition, all of the military personnel
in these transportation units would be current in rifle skills and small

unit tactics and could take their turn in the patrol duty rotations when they were not manning the convoys.

As soon as a zone has been stabilized the enlarged military police companies would maintain that stability so that the civil affairs units could establish contact with the indigenous leaders. Civil affairs units would perform as liaison to these local civilian bureaucracies, a critical and necessary function to sustain an ongoing stable local government. The civil engineering companies simultaneously would spearhead the reconstruction of the damage perpetrated upon the locals during the combat phases of the operations and the medics would treat the civilian wounded who had been injured in the combat phase. Humanitarian medical treatment would improve relations with the indigenous people.

These specific military units cannot be expected to remain in the secured area indefinitely. They must move on to the next "hot" area of operations that needs to be neutralized and secured. Therefore, other highly trained units are needed to fill-in for the advancing MPs, civil engineers, civil affairs specialists and medics. Is this the time that civilian contractors take over these responsibilities? Not in my mind, it isn't. In counter-insurgency operations even the most secure rear areas are vulnerable to attack. The follow-up units must be combat ready and subject to military disciplines such as rules of engagement, the UCMJ, etc.

ON THE UNITED STATES AIR FORCE

Over the last several months I have spent a lot of time talking about the US Army and the US Marine Corps. Both are underfunded and undermanned for the Terrorist/guerrilla war(s) that this country is facing for the next twenty to thirty years or more. The United States Air Force is, in my opinion, overfunded and overstaffed relative to the organization's mission for the next generation or so. This being the case then funding must be redirected from this service to those services that must carry the burden of this warfare that we are engaging at present and in the foreseeable future.

Since the fall of "The Evil Empire" in 1989 the requirement for rapid strategic strike forces has diminished considerably. The weapons systems supporting this strategic mission were changing rapidly even before the breakup of the USSR. The change in weapons technology was migrating since the early 1970's from manned aircraft to unmanned ground-launched ICBM's, sea-launched ICBM's, ground-launched cruise missiles (GLCM's), sea-launched cruise missiles (SLCM's) and some air-launched cruise missiles (ALCM's).

In spite of this evolution toward missiles in weapons technology, the Air Force bought two more manned bombers to replace the aging B-52. The first model was the swing-wing, supersonic B-1 that proved to be a political "hot potato" between the Republicans and the Democrats. It was designed and tested during the Nixon/Ford administrations; then shelved during the Carter administration only to be revived during the Reagan administration. When all was said and done the taxpayer was burdened with about a hundred very expensive "hanger queens" that never fulfilled its mission to replace the B-52. The B-1 has very high maintenance costs, initially due to a faulty pedestal that was central to the swing-wing design among other problems. When operational, it was often limited to subsonic flights because of design faults and due to high fuel consumption at supersonic speeds. So the B-52 remained in the inventory and continued to serve effectively.

The second attempt to replace the B-52 was a program to develop and deploy a "stealth" bomber. The designers avoided the problems of supersonic speed that they encountered with the B-1; they built the B-2 for subsonic speeds and no swing-wings. The most probable reason for these omissions is that "stealth" materials couldn't withstand the stresses from supersonics. However, now we're talking about really "big bucks". The B-2 has turned out to be the "queen" of them all. It was touted to be state-of-the-art stealth technology from its smallest inner-workings. It had a large capacity weapon's bay. It looked as if Batman and Robin were the crew members. Such a honey! Once delivered to the Air Force inventory it was to be the ultimate hit for...um...well... ah...*the Rose Parade or air shows or, or what?* And that's what the tax-payer got...a $2.25 Billion (each) aircraft without a viable combat mission! There have been a lot of "Ooohs" and "Aaahs" at the air shows and holiday parades where the B-2 makes a fly-by with more thousands of dollars spent on the maintenance, fuel, etc to send it to the venue from its home base in Missouri. But is this prudent use of our tax dollars?

Both the B-1 and B-2 saw limited action in both Gulf Wars. Early on, however, the B-2 was flying its combat mission non-stop from Missouri to the Middle East and back. This meant over thirty hours of flying that included several aerial refuelings for every sortie. Why? There are at least a couple of reasons. First, the Air Force spent so much money on this aircraft that it didn't want to risk losing one by having it stationed outside of the United States. This seems to be a common practice these days. The aircraft are so expensive that the military is reluctant to expose them to risk; so they stay at home while the older airframes do the work. In the meantime, the expensive, state-of-the-art equipment grows obsolete sitting safely out of harm's way. But most important, the stealth technology of the B-2 aircraft is so fragile that it cannot stand the weather in the Middle East or its closest appropriate air base at Diego Garcia. The aircraft is so insubstantial that it must be housed in an air conditioned hanger whenever it's on the ground. Even rain is damaging to the skin of this technological dog. Is this really the equipment that we want to have in the very harsh environment that war is?

At today's values these two aircraft with limited capability and fragile design have cost over $100 Billion (that's a **"B"**) to the taxpayer! As these "national treasures" grow obsolete on the ground or at the fly-bys in Pasadena, the venerable B-52 continues to perform the combat mission, just as it has for over the last 50 years. That's right; the B-52 became operational in 1952. The last model rolled off the assembly line in 1962. This bomber worked as a nuclear high altitude delivery weapon and a nuclear low level delivery vehicle during the Cold War, a conventional (iron) bomb delivery aircraft in Vietnam, Gulf War I and the Iraq War and Afghanistan War and an aerial launch platform for cruise missiles and smart bombs in Iraq and Afghanistan. Arguably it is the best combat aircraft ever built. In my opinion, the BUFF (The moniker given to the B-52 during the Vietnam War; it's the acronym for "Big-Ugly-Fat-Fellow".) should be the established standard for all future combat aircraft. It was relatively inexpensive to develop (in 1947), build and maintain and it has had a long, varied and distinguished service life. It is an old aircraft now and ready to be retired. But the B-52 legacy of efficacy should live on. Does the Air Force do this? Not on your life!

The latest Air Force combat aircraft is the F-22 Raptor. It is supersonic, with built-in stealth technology and **it costs nearly $200 million per copy**! We have received 181 Raptors as of this date at a cost to the taxpayer of over $36 Billion. Has the Air Force sent them to the war in the Middle East to support our troops? NO! The F-22 is *too expensive to risk in war!* Besides the expense, the F-22 doesn't have a CAS (close air support) capability. The stealth technology of the F-22 is designed to penetrate the "Evil Empire's" radar defense so that the aircraft can dogfight the supersonic Soviet fighters. Hello! The Soviet Union collapsed nearly 20 years ago and there hasn't been an aerial dogfight by the USAF for 30 years or more! Does this scenario have a familiar ring to it? You bet it does. Instead of combat missions, the F-22 flies over the Super bowl in diamond formation in 2008. I am sure this mission would create Ooohs and Aaahs but the bowl dome was closed so the spectators couldn't even see them. Now there's some well spent tax dollars. Meanwhile, the older F-15s, F-16s, F-18s and A-10s are doing the real work.

A few months ago a F-15 disintegrated in the air on a routine stateside sortie. The entire F-15 fleet was grounded while inspectors determined the cause of the accident and whether or not all other F-15s had the same structural flaw. Sure enough, metal fatigue in a fuselage component had caused the problem and the oldest 30% of the fleet showed signs of the same weakness. The newer airframes were released to fly again but the older one-third of this aircraft were permanently grounded; a prudent decision. But the other two-thirds of the fleet were released to fly again when no flaws were found in their airframes. The Air Force response to this permanent grounding of 140 or so of the older F-15s came through the public comments of Air Combat Commander, General John D.W. Corley. He demanded that a follow-on order of F-22 Raptors be purchased to replace the grounded F-15s. So the taxpayer is supposed to shell out another $29 Billion to cover this requirement that can't satisfy the current needs of CAS in the Middle East?

The prudent solution is to build more airframes of existing F-16s and A-10s and stuff them with current electronics to cover the needs of the CAS mission (A-10s would be best suited for this.) in the Middle East and the high altitude air-to-air mission (F-16s would be best suited, but this aircraft performs CAS very well too!) for homeland security. The cost savings would be humongous. In addition to the cost saving in building more of existing aircraft, the Air Force could save another bundle by concentrating on unmanned drone technology. These systems cost about $10 Million each (probably $15 Million now with inflation). This sum gets the taxpayer the ground control system that controls the aircraft from half-a-world away and three fully equipped airframes. With drones the Air Force saves on pilot training, survival/egress equipment, billeting costs for aircrew, pay, allowances, benefits and retirement of aircrew and a myriad of other expenses.

Another traditional mission stepchild of the Air Force is air mobility and search and rescue (SAR). After WWII the operational aircraft commands were SAC (bombers and tankers), TAC (fighters) and MAC (transport aircraft). In the 1990's the air force reduced the three commands into two with bombers and fighters in Air Combat Command and transports, aerial tankers and search and rescue in Air Mobility Command. This made good sense but the hierarchy of the service was still controlled by the fighter and bomber generals. As a result the Air Mobility Command remained second class to the "hunter/killers" of Air Combat Command. But air mobility/aerial refueling has had just as distinguished an history as the bombers and fighters. The aircraft are just not as sexy looking! One can suggest the heroics of transports during WWII in Operation Overlord, Market Garden, the Italian campaign, the Burma Hump. The tankers saved any number of fighters and bombers running low on fuel after missions over North Vietnam and virtually saved the aircraft and crews. Search and Rescue units, always a sub-command in military airlift/mobility have saved hundreds if not thousands of lives of aircrew in war as well as hundreds of civilians in natural disasters. If any aircrew deserves the Bushian swagger, normally associated with the fighter pilot, it's the paramedic on the SAR helicopter.

With the decline of the importance of Cold War strategic bomber missions and air-to-air fighter combat, air mobility, with the need for rapid deployment of troops and supplies to regional combat areas and the rapid deployment of CAS fighters to support these troops, has increased in importance to the Air Force's 21st Century order of battle. Certainly during this first decade and for the next twenty years or so of this century, air mobility must be considered a priority command. If more aircraft are to be purchased and more squadrons are to be expanded, the hierarchy of the Air Force should seriously consider more C-17s, C-130s, air refueling tankers and SAR fixed-wing and helicopter aircraft.

The role of the Air Force has changed considerably in the counterinsurgency era. Experience has proved that air power does not destroy the will of the enemy to resist. It doesn't stop production of war making capabilities; and it certainly doesn't sever supply lines of transnational organizations or nation-states. Air-to-air combat is history. Strategic bombing is history. Where the Air Force can best be utilized, in a counterinsurgency era is in a support role with a mission priority list such as follows:

- Close Air Support (CAS) of the ground forces (F-16/A-10/Predator drone)
- Rapid air deployment (Transport) of ground forces to combat zones (C-17/C-130)

- Air supply to combat forces (Transport) (C-130/C-17)
- Air refueling for all manned CAS aircraft and long range air transports (KC 135/KC-10/KC-130/scheduled replacement for the KC-135)
- Search and Rescue squadrons (fixed wing and helicopter aircraft)
- Special Operations (C-130/AC-130/helicopters of several models)
- Air superiority fighter squadrons held at current levels and reduced as older aircraft are retired. (F-15/F-16/ F-22-as delivered in current contract of 181)
- Homeland security/border control drone squadrons increased as required to protect the Zone Interior
- Strategic Missile squadrons reduced as these ground based ICBMs are retired
- Strategic bomber squadrons reduced (B-1/B-2 aircraft reduced on an accelerated schedule)
- Space Command held static with existing satellite inventory
- Cyber-space units (?) if it is necessary but without increasing overall manpower of the Air Force

However, the bottom line is that the Air Force, isn't interested in a support role or fighting the current Counterinsurgency/guerrilla war because it just doesn't fit the fighter pilot's style or ego. This is unacceptable behavior for the commanders of a very expensive military service. They must adjust their equipment requirements and mission goals to the realities of the current battlefield and enthusiastically support the most advantageous role for the good of the country.

ON THE UNITED STATES NAVY

Let us continue our dialogue on how to change the mindset of our traditional armed forces so that they can operate effectively in a counter-insurgency environment. Over the last month Robert Gates, the US Secretary of Defense, has chastised the Air Force and the US Army for not vigorously responding to the needs of the troops in the Afghanistan and Iraq combat zones regarding proper equipment. At the Air War College at Maxwell Air Force Base he noted that much too much time was spent planning strategies and tactics and procuring systems for a future war that may never happen. Actually, what he was pointing out to the senior officers was that they were really reliving the WW II/Cold War scenario where large conventional forces slugged it out on expansive battlefields with main battle tanks, swift troop maneuvers and massed artillery barrages; while overhead pointy-nosed supersonic fighters fought to the death one-on-one with evil enemy pilots; and stealthy bombers penetrated deep into the enemy mother country to obliterate the war making industries and bring the populace to its knees. ***It just isn't going to happen!***

Secretary Gates said much what I have said about the lack of creative forward thinking in the US Army and US air Force, but to this date I haven't heard him pouncing on the Navy for similar sins. In my opinion, the Navy is not without sin in this regard either. Its one saving grace may be due to the fact that the Marine Corps are a part of the Navy Department, so the sailors skate under the radar of criticism with the Marines running interference. The actual "ship Navy", however, lacks every bit as much as the Air Force when one measures the organization for creative planning, strategies, tactics and weapons procurement. As their sister services are doing, the Navy is living in WW II/Cold War history, skipping the present non-polar international environment where small guerrilla/insurgent wars are the order of the day, and *dreaming* of the return of the romantic era of great fleets fighting the single decisive battle for control of the seas. Needless to say, **WAKE UP, NAVY**- *this just isn't going to happen either!*

The United States Navy must focus on the present and near future (the next 10 to 20 years) and procure the appropriate weapons systems to overcome insurgency operations. Furthermore, strategic and tactical plans must be modified to meet these small war challenges. This unconventional combat role places the sea Navy in a secondary support role for the success of the US Marine Corps. Also, the Navy has to make much greater effort to support the other services, particularly the US Army, so that it can efficaciously respond to the dangers of a rapidly evolving non-polar international environment[7].

This metamorphous is unfamiliar to traditionalists. The traditional nation-state is no longer the only operative in international power and military response must adapt to this new international environment.

Currently, the most viable military scenario, both on land or at sea is a low-intensity, guerrilla/insurgency. This military scenario is the most likely over the next ten, twenty and even thirty years. The United States Navy needs to respond to this environment by adjusting their order of battle. The Navy does not need to maintain its current level of nuclear submarines, nor does it need as many super carriers, or missile cruisers and destroyers. What it does need is more rapid response, expeditionary attack troop transport/VTOL(TT/VTOL) carriers to move Marines and SEALS to local areas of low intensity conflicts and adequately supply these troops as well as small; and swift corsair class

---

[7] Non-polar international environment: The international system is in rapid flux from a "unipolar" single superpower world to a diffused concentration of power. Non-polar differs from traditional multi-polar of the early 20th Century in that multi-polarity connotes an oligarchy of balanced nation-states. The non-polar international environment provides for power to be diffused both vertically and horizontally. It not only recognizes power among the traditional nation-states, but also power incorporated in transnational organizations including al-Qaeda, Hamas, Hezbollah and the Islamic Jihad. It even includes the multi-national political organizations such as the United Nations, NATO, the Organization of American States; and even humanitarian organizations such as the Bill and Malinda Gates Foundation, Doctors without Borders, etc. and economic organizations such as OPEC and the G-Eight. (Read: Richard Haass' article "The Age of Nonpolarity", *Foreign Affairs*, Vol. 87, number 3; May/June 2008, pages 44-56.)

ships to combat the guerrilla speedboats like the ones that damaged the USS Cole and harass our off-shore support fleet. There is the nucleus for this type of service already in existence; it just needs to be expanded upon. Like the evolution from the "battleship" mentality in the early stages of WW II inhibiting the newer "aircraft carrier" vision among the admirals; so the "aircraft carrier and submarine" admirals of today are inhibiting the realization of a rapid response-expeditionary-troop-attack fleet. This counter-insurgency configuration, as a major strategy, is a foreign mindset to the current decision making powers in the US Navy and it must change.

By dumping submarine, super-carrier and some fighter aircraft contracts, the Navy would release billions for the expansion of a viable counter-insurgency fleet. Furthermore, there would more funding available to expand the Marine Corps.

The counter-insurgency fleet is nothing new in the US Navy. As a fact, it has been the primary configuration for most of the service's history. The USS Constitution ("Old Ironsides" to some of you readers) and her sisters were the largest warships in the US Navy for many years. The USS Constitution was of the frigate class. Most of the ships in the US Navy were even smaller sloops or coastal gun boats or barges. The United States simply had no "ships of the line". During the Civil War and in the later 19th Century we added small fleets of river boats to patrol the major rivers here in America as well as the Yangtze and Yellow Rivers in China. It was only in the 20th century that the United States, with the influential doctrine of AT Mahan and the energy of Theodore Roosevelt, established itself as a major sea power. Of course, this philosophy served us well through WW II and the Cold War. But all of this is history and we have to adjust our thinking to the 21st Century. So, the United States Navy must evolve in the following manner:

- Acquire and deploy Troop transport/VTOL carrier groups to the crisis regions in the world.
- Each Troop transport/VTOL carrier would contain one super battalion of marines that includes infantry, combat engineers, light armor and light artillery. On the carrier deck would be attack helicopters, transport helicopters and VTOL fighters.
- The swift agile Corsair class fighting ships would protect the TT/VTOL carriers with ample automatic Gatling Guns, laser-

guided surface-to-surface and surface-to-air missiles and other weapon systems to adequately engage swift guerrilla or suicide boats.

- All ships of the group should be equipped with area surveillance radar and sonar technology to insure identification of friend or foe (IFF) at a range sufficient to evade or engage successfully. (In counter-insurgency operations evasion may be the tactic of choice depending on the political circumstances.)
- A sufficient number of corsair class ships must be deployed to protect the TT/VTOL carriers, and the necessary supply ships assigned to support the cruise requirements and initial combat needs of the group.
- Under differing circumstances, more than one TT/VTOL carrier may be assigned to the group as well as more standard troop ships with added infantry. Of course, our existing super-carriers also may be added for more air support depending on the situation.

The key is flexibility in getting "boots on the ground" with adequate supporting firepower to engage a guerrilla enemy.

ON JUS IN BELLO

Several weeks ago (April 2008) General Petraeus and Ambassador Crocker returned to Washington to brief the President, Congress and, to a lesser extent, the American people on the successes of the troop surge of the last six months. By all accounts the increased troop deployment has reduced the violence in Iraq. Both American casualties and civilian collateral casualties have fallen in a near dramatic fashion. That is, until the renewed violence of the more recent weeks. Even as Petraeus and Crocker were cautiously briefing the reductions in bloodshed, the Shiites blasted into Basra. To the north in Baghdad there were terror attacks in Sadr City and the Green Zone was pummeled at will by the insurgents. Al-Sadr proclaimed that his moratorium on assaults was over and he was releasing his Mahdi Militia to continue the fight for liberation from the occupying American forces. The newly constituted Iraqi Government army responded to the clashes. They *failed!* Hundreds, perhaps thousands deserted in the face of fire, if they even got that close to the action. American forces had to be dispatched to the skirmishes. We are no closer to getting out of the Iraq mess than we were six months ago.

Has the surge worked? If so, is it permanent or temporary? Are there other factors in play during this time period that has impacted the reduction in violence? Well, let's look at a list of all of the violence containment factors.

IRAQI VIOLENCE CONTAINMENT FACTORS

1. The United States troop surge in 2007 of 5 brigades (21,000 to 28,000 soldiers including the additional support troops). The purpose is to reduce violence to a minimum in Baghdad

so that our puppet Iraqi government could coordinate power between the religious factions that have divided the region (for hundreds of years) and most recently the country of Iraq (for 87 years) between the Sunnis, Shiites and Kurds.

2. Al-Sadr's six-month ceasefire/truce of his Mahdi Militia in early 2007 and the recent extension of that cease fire. This self-imposed ceasefire has been monumental in reducing violence in Iraq. But it was not of our doing!

3. The building of walls separating the neighborhoods in Baghdad and the assignment of similar sectarians to the applicable neighborhood. This is essentially an apartheid solution and basically violates the United States' philosophy of integration and humanitarian mandates.

4. The recent alliance of some Iraqi tribal leaders to the United States and their abandonment of their alliance to the al-Qaeda faction now located in the country. Middle East tribal cultures are very loose with their alliances as the United States found to be true in the Afghanistan Northern Alliance war against the Taliban in 2002. They tend to change alliances as often as their socks.

5. The agreement between the United States' puppet Iraqi government with the Iranian government to stop the flow of arms and particularly the IED materials to the guerrilla/insurgent forces in Iraq. Behind the saber-rattling theatrics of the Bush Administration, quiet but productive diplomacy prevailed to save hundreds of lives in the streets of Baghdad.

QUESTIONS: Is there sufficient evidence that the **surge** has been the most effective factor of the five listed above? Does the reduction in violence that has occurred over the last several months constitute a permanent reduction in violence? Is the recent alliance with the tribal leaders permanent? Has the United States' puppet Iraqi government made the necessary conciliatory proposals with the two Islamic sects represented in the government?

Let's continue our quest for answers by revisiting the Principles of Terrorist War to see if that can shed any light on this matter.

In both of my books, *The War Lectures 1861-1865* and *The Prai-*

rie Wars 1840-1890, I discussed the principles of war and pointed out that the guerrilla/insurgency/terror genre of conflict also had some unique maxims that must always be considered. I named this unique principium the "four ts" of terror. In spite of the common view that terrorists and guerrillas are a mob of raggedy-assed, poorly armed zealots with a fervor that far out weighs common sense, these organized groups have been able to stifle the best of armies. Guerrilla/terror warfare has always been with us but for some strange reason the militaries of cities, countries, alliances and empires over the centuries seem to have disregarded the substance of this type of conflict.

Once again the United States is fighting a guerrilla/terrorist adversary. I say, once again, because this is certainly not the first time in our history. The Native-Americans fought guerrilla style against us in colonial times, during the Seminole wars in the Florida swamps and on the prairies of the western frontier. The American colonists fought guerrilla style against the British in the Revolutionary War under leaders such as Marion, Moultrie and even Washington. There were guerrilla units in the Missouri/Kansas region during the American Civil War under William Quantrill. John Singleton Mosley used guerrilla tactics behind Union lines in Virginia. The Confederate cavalry under JEB Stuart, Nathan Bedford Forrest, John Hunt Morgan, and Joseph Wheeler disrupted the efficacy of the federal armies by attacking communication lines leading to the Union front. The US Army fought a guerrilla war in the Philippines from 1899-1902. The British, our ally at that time, used guerrilla tactics against the Turks under the leadership of T. E. Lawrence in WWI. The Yugoslavs used guerrilla tactics against the Nazis in WWII; as did the Polish underground and the French resistance and these organizations received assistance from the US military to sustain their activities during this great tragedy. With that association, the US commanders became very familiar with guerrilla/terrorist tactics.

As I have mentioned in previous essays, Mao Zedong, Che Guevara, Ho Chi Minh, wrote late Twentieth Century books on the tactics of guerrilla/insurgency warfare. To some degree or another, all of the examples mentioned above used the "Four ts" for their strategic planning and execution. So what are these "four ts"? I prefer to set up a verbal equation: **TERRORIST WAR = time + terrain/topography**

+ tenacity + terror/torture (as in terrifying atrocities). These four strategic elements level the battlefield between a large, well equipped, conventionally/traditionally trained, nation/state army and a guerrilla/ terrorist band. So let's take each "t" in detail.

- **Time**: A guerrilla/terrorist is fighting for a fundamental idea, such as preserving a traditional lifestyle or creating greater opportunities to determine their own destiny. Their adversary is a foreign imperialist nation, or an elitist class ensconced in the terrorist's home region. Both are there to extract material wealth, resources and/or human labor from the indigenous population. The terrorist/guerrillas and their leaders are the underpaid, underappreciated and overworked victims. These common people want more control of their property, their community resources and their destiny. This said, these people are not going anywhere else to fight for their perceived natural, rights nor do they have any timetable to complete their Herculean task. Time is on their side! The guerrilla soldier is unpaid. The terrorist is on no rotation schedule to go home; because he is already there. A prime example of this "time strategy" was Ho Chi Minh's timetable for the Vietnam War. He, his leaders, and the Vietnamese people were prepared to continue the war into the 1990's and beyond. They didn't have to, however. The United States gave up in 1973. Uncle Ho beat his time schedule by 15 to 20 years!

- **Terrain/topography**: The contested topography is usually the local surroundings of the guerrilla/insurgent bands. As a result the guerrilla soldier has intimate knowledge of all terrain/ topographical features in the locale, such as mountains, arroyos, caves, forest stands, streams, lakes, water holes, etc. In the local cities, towns and villages the guerrilla knows where all of the safe-houses are located; where escape tunnels and spider-holes have been dug; what sewers can be used for human movement, etc. The knowledge of all of these features also levels the battle area for the insurgent against the foreign adversary. Of course, the guerrillas normally operate among their friends or neighbors too. The assistance of these indigenous civilians helps the guerrilla enormously with supplies, arms, ammunition, intelligence and warnings of danger.

- **Tenacity**: The guerrilla/insurgent is extremely patient and very persistent. He has the conviction that the mission is sacred. His life, customs and culture are at stake, so the terrorist is resigned to fight to the death or for a lifetime. The insurgent pursues his goals with a resoluteness that overcomes extremes in human suffering. The reader only needs to research the trials, defeats, tribulations of the Viet Cong during their long wars against the Japanese, French and the Americans to appreciate the value of this strategic principle.

- **Terror/torture** (as in terrifying atrocities): Death/execution is absolute. Pain is feared. Painful death/execution in the human psyche is brutal. Because this painful death/execution process is so atrocious, it can be used to great effect as a weapon against an enemy. Torturous death has a shock value that can persuade the foreign witnesses to give up the fight. Contrary to the hype of the media stories, the Islamic terrorists have not demonstrated diabolical torturous executions when compared to some of the practices that have been used in past history. As a matter of fact their public executions by beheading that the Western World views as so horrific are essentially the normal mode of execution in Middle East Islamic countries. This beheading is swift and perhaps, less painful than hanging, electrocution or lethal injection. The Islamic terrorists have simply begun to use television to expand the public viewing. The hundreds of civilian corpses found in the streets of Baghdad are a different matter, but from what I gather these victims were most often shot in the head. Not all of these victims, by any means, showed pre-mortem abuse. A shot to the head is usually swift and relatively painless. If the Jihadist really wanted to be cruel, there is a lot of latitude to adjust methodology. (To really understand horrific torturous death, one needs to compare the torture practices of the Islamic terrorists to the Comanche Indians on the American frontier in the nineteenth century. These folks had some really diabolical, torturous deaths for their captives. Another case to examine is the horrific acts of torture the Viet Cong devised to kill their captive enemy soldiers. The screams of pain sent a fearful message to all other enemy soldiers within earshot.)

The bottom line question to this terrorist principle is, "Does terror/torture work?" I think yes and no. (How's that for a waffle?) Torture/terror is less effective on highly trained combat troops. It is more effective on an unfriendly, indigenous, civilian population or a population not committed to the terrorist cause. The public execution will, at least, neutralize the people to the war effort. Torture of military prisoners for intelligence gathering purposes, on the other hand, has proven to be ineffective, because an individual combat soldier has very little or very temporary information that could be useful to the captors. When confronted with pain and suffering the prisoner will give misinformation to avoid or reduce this pain and suffering. If the torture to the military prisoner is within earshot of the prisoner's buddies, his screams may have a limited unnerving, demoralizing effect, however.

In Iraq we must be prepared to continue the fight for an extended period of time. The mistake of attacking Iraq is now a moot point. Morally, we now have the obligation to restore the country to some level of stability and security. The problem lays with the 1300 year conflict between the Shih's and Sunni's; the Kurd's and the Shih's, Sunni's and the Turks; and the former Ba'ath Party members and the non-former Ba'ath Party members. To even suggest that the current reduction in violence is a sign of significant progress to stability and security is naive. Remember, **the principle of time** is on the insurgent's side. One, two or even six months of diminished activities aren't much when compared to 1300 years of hate!

In Afghanistan the "Four ts" are also working against us. I may think that we understand the tenacity of Osama bin Laden and his leader cadre. But do we? There is no evidence that they plan to surrender, nor do any of their followers. They have an open end time table of *forever*, or until they're *dead*. Therefore, we'll have to seek out their caves and kill them, or at least, the great majority of them. But this won't be easy. Just look at a map where al-Qaeda is suspected to be holed up. The Border Mountains between Afghanistan and Pakistan has the "best of the best" in *topography* for guerrilla warfare. The area is sparsely populated, but most of the indigenous tribes are friendly to al-Qaeda or at least neutral to their cause. Roads are few; some are not more than goat paths. These hills and mountains are rugged, rocky and arid. The area encompasses hundreds, if not thousands of caves that are easily concealed from satellite or aerial detection. If discovered, these hideouts are difficult for an armed force to approach. Their depth in the ground and the angle of their entrances relative to the side of the mountains make them impervious to aerial attack except, perhaps, with bunker-buster, laser-guided ordnance. We have some bunker-buster bombs, but we don't have thousands of them and we don't have an efficient delivery system. Furthermore, we must identify the occupied caves from the unoccupied ones. This is accomplished by "boots-on-the-ground"! It will take a large contingent of Special Ops forces to meet this need. We don't have this large contingent of Special Forces, however, because Special Forces and guerrilla warfare have been neglected by the military hierarchy, forever and always. As I have said before, we have a long row to hoe.

So far Petraeus has been correct; and the surge has worked. I was wrong in the essay written several months ago when the surge was first announced. However, he said that the surge would be a temporary fix, perhaps six to eight months, but by then the al-Maliki government will have to step forward and assert effective authority to bring order, safety and security to the country. The time is up! Our troops have done their job and they have done a good job. Now it is up to the Iraqis.

On a more important note, however, the insurgents are in control of the battle area. They can start or stop the war at their leisure! The Petraeus strategy has worked for what it was supposed to do. But the US State Department's portion of the task has failed. The Iraqi government has failed.

"RIGHT" JUDGMENT; FLAWED LOGIC; SHODDY HISTORIOGRAPHY

The Heller decision supports what the American Rifle Association and the constructionist right-wing maintain that the Second Amendment guarantees the right of the individual citizen to **own** firearms. The "operative" words upon which they base their argument are "…the right of the people to keep and bear arms, shall not be infringed." In spite of the fact that "people" is a collective noun they insist that "to keep and bear arms" is an individual's right. Omitted from their argument, however, are some critical issues relating to other words in this controversial amendment. Such words as "well regulated" and "Militia" that precede that final phrase, or in Justice Scalia's opinion, relegated to a "prefatory clause" and summarily dismissed as superfluous by virtue of a linguistic technicality. These words, indeed this whole "prefatory clause" that the justice so casually dismisses as meaningless drivel **must** be carefully examined for the words' specific meanings and relevance of the clause, prefatory or not, within the context of the late Eighteenth Century when the amendment was drafted and debated.

The **United States Constitution** is not, and was never meant to be, a freshman English essay. It is, and was written to be the most basic legal/historical document in American jurisprudence to defend the citizenry from the **tyrannies of an oppressive central government**. Justice Scalia's dismissal of 48% of the verbiage ("A well regulated Militia, being necessary to the security of a free State…") of this Second Amendment based on a 20th Century linguistic technicality is, in my opinion, absurd! The author of the Second Amendment, James Madison, was not a linguistics scholar; he was the author/father of the **United States Constitution and the Bill of Rights** and, by virtue of his authorship was and still should be considered the best (United States) constitutional law expert in all human history. Mr. Madison would have had to clearly expect the words "well regulated" and "Militia" to impact the "*operative*" clause! To dismiss or even to trivialize this "prefatory" clause consisting of 48% of the wording of this fundamental right 218 years later is intellectually disingenuous.

During those early times constabularies, police, marshals and sheriffs were few and far between in the townships and counties of the young republic. There was no central government with an established regular army and, quite honestly, the citizens were very hesitant to support a regular army because of their experiences with the British Army during the colonial era. The fledgling country had recently concluded an eight year revolutionary war against a tyrannical central government that had abused the individual and collective freedoms of the colonial citizens who had always considered themselves English citizens. Now that the United States was free from the shackles of the English Crown, the fathers of the Revolution were free to come up with their own standards of "fair" government. However, the rule of law had to be upheld in these far flung communities and protection from the indigenous tribes and aggressive wild beasts had to be maintained. To thwart this danger from hostile natives, wild beasts or a tyrannical and overly powerful Federal Government the leaders of some of the several states came together at a common convention and/or within their jurisdictions to construct a foundation to protect the citizenry.

Between 1776 and 1791 several state constitutions *and* The Articles of Confederation of the United States (1778) were created to provide for a weak central government with the states retaining strong authorities over the populace. The concept of local "well regulated militia" organizations that were included in several state constitutions and later in the Articles of Confederation and finally in the United States Constitution was recognized as the fundamental protection force for the seaboard as well as the frontier communities. Of course, some of the mature counties, cities and towns along the seaboard already supported constabularies, marshals, police and/or sheriffs to handle civilian crimes and civil disobediences. The well regulated militias in these mature coastal communities were reserved for defense from hostile outside forces or a tyrannical central government. On the other hand, many of the frontier communities didn't have the luxury of full-time or even part-time sworn officers of the law, such as constables, sheriffs or marshals. Therefore, these communities, at least on occasion, had their "well regulated militia" serve the residents in the capacity of these sworn officers of the law in addition to protection from outside hostile forces, such as hostile indigenous tribes, which, I might add, was a very real threat to these communities.

So what does "Militia" mean? (Be mindful that this term is spelled with a capital "M" in the Second Amendment.) At one point in the decision, Justice Scalia opines that since the term "Militia" was limited to only able-bodied men between the ages of eighteen and forty-five, the term constituted only a subset of the people and, therefore as a word representing only a part of the whole, Militia, could not linguistically modify the word "people" in the operative clause of this Amendment. But, let's look at this from a practical and a historical perspective. The phrase "well regulated *Militia*" requires examination in the same light as the term *people* does in the context of the late 18th century. At this time in our history the electorate only consisted of white free men over the age of twenty-one and in some instances required the ownership of 20 acres of land and a mule. Life expectancy for the white male was somewhere between 35 and 40. Additionally, "able-bodied" at that time did not mean that an individual had to meet the physical requirements of 21st century soldiering; it meant only to be able to physically place a musket to the shoulder even if one couldn't stand up! Militia participation in the early American communities required that *all* able-bodied men must register for the local militia and drill in the manual of arms periodically (constituting "well-regulated") as prescribed by the authority of that local community. This participation included white men, black men, invalid men (who could shoulder a musket, that is) and those that didn't own 20 acres and a mule. Justice Scalia only mentions age limits of 18-45, when, in fact, the townships, counties or the colonies varied their age requirements depending on the size of force that could be mustered from the existing populace to respond to the severity of the threat presented. The requirement that all able-bodied men must register for the local militia to protect the community from all outside threats or local disobediences as necessary, occasionally meant all males between sixteen and sixty, or between fifteen and fifty as well as between eighteen and forty-five. Since the life expectancy of the white male was under sixty or fifty or even forty-five for this matter, and the voting age and full membership into the body politic was twenty-one in 1789 when this Amendment was written and "able-bodied male" meant any male that could physically lift a musket to his shoulder, black men who couldn't vote and non-propertied white men that were disenfranchised, arguably then, the term "Militia" effectively included the vast, vast majority (perhaps as much as over 99%) of the male population of the times. Therefore, it is difficult to reason that the local militias were ***subsets*** of the body politic; more appropriately the local militias were ***supersets*** of the body politic and, contrary to Justice Scalia's opinion on the term in question, "Militia" **is a proper modifier** of the *collective noun* "people".

Many communities built armories (or arsenals as they were often called in those days) to store the necessary arms, rations and other military accoutrements for the people registered for militia service. These buildings were often surrounded by a defensive stockade where the local citizenry could congregate for collective protection in times of grave crisis. However, there were a substantial number of communities that felt they did not have the financial or material wherewithal to build a community armory. In this situation the common protocol in these communities was to have the able-bodied male citizens keep a firearm, accoutrements and rations in their homes and respond, ready and equipped to defend the community, at the established warning signal. Therefore, in the time of the development of the language in the several state constitutions, the Articles of Confederation and, eventually, the United States Constitution with its associated Bill of Rights, the community Militias and their equipment were garrisoned by two distinctly different practices. With this in mind it appears to me that Madison, when he wrote the draft for the amendment related to bearing arms, he was addressing the community militia need, albeit, with both practices of garrisoning a militia and its equipment in mind.

When the several states found that they were struggling to survive separately under the Articles of Confederation, decisions were made to convene, in conference, to debate and conceive an instrument that would provide a stronger bind among the several states for mutual justice, general welfare, defense and commerce. This conference in May 1787 was initially joined by seven of the thirteen states, but by the end of the convention in September of that same year delegates from twelve of the states were involved. (Only Rhode Island failed to join in the conference.) In the course of the debates for a stronger system of centralized fundamental law for the young country, the United States Constitution was conceived. There was considerable discourse by the delegates between the powers of the perceived central government and the powers to be reserved for the several state governments. Only after much anguish were compromises on these several issues between the two factions devised. Even after this basic historic document was completed, insecurities of the states and the populace remained. It still was not clear in the minds of many that the basic language of the document sufficiently guaranteed the rights that the citizens believed to be their rights as former Englishmen and that state law was equal or superior to the central laws.

By 1789 James Madison, considered the author of the main document and arguably one of the premier attorneys in America, expert in English law and by that virtue, Blackstone, as well, was hard at work, pretty much in solitary, by the way, developing a series of amendments to clarify the ambiguities that were causing the insecurities among the state governments and the citizenry. He borrowed language from several of the state constitutions *in existence at the time* and the Articles of Confederation for twelve amendments that he thought would satisfy the criticisms that he had received. Essentially ten of these twelve statements became the first amendments of the new Constitution and designated the Bill of Rights upon ratification in 1791. But one must not forget that the states were equal or perceived superior to the federal laws until the Fourteenth Amendment was ratified in July, 1868 seventy-seven years later. There was no reason, initially, for the citizenry to feel threatened by the limitations of the federal Second Amendment when their state constitutions broadened this right to self-defense. Justice Scalia ignores this point.

According to Leonard W. Levy, Mellon Professor Emeritus of Claremont Graduate School, Madison, took the phraseology from the Pennsylvania Constitution of 1776 for the amendment related to the "right of the people to keep and bear arms". He goes on to expound that since Pennsylvania did not have a state militia at the time of the writing of that Pennsylvania Constitution, the phrase "the right to bear arms" could not be relegated to a military connotation as so many liberal councilors suggest in their arguments that the Second Amendment protects the States' rights to have an armed force for collective protection against hostiles, foreign or domestic. Justice Scalia supports Levy on this point.

However, Professor Levy fails to point out that the words "well regulated" and "militia" came from the **Virginia Constitution's Declaration of Rights** that was adopted in that state about the same time in 1776 as the Pennsylvania Constitution was adopted and the Virginia document was authored by George Mason, a close collaborator of none other than Mr. James Madison, the author of the United States Constitution and the Bill of Rights. Furthermore, the fact that Pennsylvania did not refer to the terms "militia" or "military" could have been due to the *strong influence* of the **Religious Society of Friends** that rejected the concepts of "war" and "militarism" and deliberately omitted such terminologies from several official state documents but still adhered to a body of *trained and registered* persons to protect against hostile forces. Also, there was no intrinsic reason to include this term "militia" in the Pennsylvania State Constitution or its other state documents since during that time of their composition most, if not all, *"well regulated militias"* were relegated to the citizenry on a more *local* basis; that is a county, town or hamlet.

In my opinion, Professor Levy's claim based on *omissions* in the text of the Pennsylvania Constitution is weak. He wasn't there at the time and to my knowledge there is no specific documentation suggesting what he professes. Madison, on the other hand, was a Virginian and had a substantial influence in developing the Virginia Constitution and the associated Declaration of Rights in 1776. The Virginia document did use the phrase "That a *well regulated militia, composed of the body of the people, trained to arms*, is the proper, natural, and safe defense of a *free state....* " It is interesting to note that Justice Scalia avoids even a mention of the Virginia Constitution or the associated Declaration of Rights when he argues for implication of the collective noun "people" to connote "individual". However, the verbiage in the Virginia Con-

stitution and its associated Declaration of Rights was drafted within
a matter of weeks of the Pennsylvania Constitution; so why wouldn't
Madison have used the phraseology in the state Constitutional documents for which he was most familiar? Common sense strongly suggests that he would. Furthermore, an early draft of Madison's proposed
"to bear arms" amendment (i.e. the US Second Amendment) includes
"composed of the body of the People..." in the text and clearly refers
to a collective group to be a *"well regulated militia"*. Justice Scalia
rejects drafts that challenge his train of thought.

As a final comment, Levy's claims have not been sustained by the
American Bar Association, the American Civil Liberties Union or the
findings in 1967 of the President's Commission on Law Enforcement
and Administration of Justice. This President's Commission stated in
1967, "The U.S. Supreme Court and lower Federal courts have consistently interpreted this (Second) Amendment *only* as a prohibition
against Federal interference with State militias and *not* as a guarantee
of an individual's right to keep and carry arms." Many gun enthusiasts (and with this most recent decision that we discuss in this essay,
the conservative justices of the current United States Supreme Court)
disagree with this interpretation. Therefore, let me continue without
prejudice.

In Federalist #46, Madison argues for the continued **dominance
of the states** over **a federal government**. In this argument he alludes
to **armed state militias as a necessary means to guarantee the states'
necessary protection from a tyrannical government**. Federalist #46
does not address personal ownership of arms for self protection. Again
this clearly shows that Madison drafted the "to bear arms" amendment
for the US Constitution based on his knowledge of the Virginia Constitution's Declaration of Rights, supported by his beliefs for the need
of *vigilance from tyranny of a central government* by using such language as "well regulated, trained in arms" citizen "militia". However at
the time of his writing, one can surmise that he prudently used some of
the Pennsylvania Constitution's verbiage for at least a couple of legitimate political reasons; (1) to give the State of Pennsylvania a sense of
contribution and, perhaps, politically to gain the delegation's approval
and (2) the Pennsylvania phraseology was less wordy than the Virginia
document's phraseology. In my opinion, the phrase "the right of the

people to keep and bear arms" clearly has a substantive connection to "a well regulated militia [composed of the body of the people]".

Justice Scalia ignores Madison's and the other founding fathers' motivations on this matter of protecting the citizenry from a federal tyranny. He insists on focusing on linguistics *form* to the detriment of historical *substance*[8]. By doing this, he travels a circuitous discourse to arrive at his presupposed conclusion. For example, Scalia reasons that nine states in the union between the dates of 1789 and 1820 include the word "self-defense" in their textual clause "to keep and bear arms". Therefore, the justice opines that if these nine states included the word self-defense in their operative clause, ergo the federal Second Amendment phraseology of the textual clause, "to keep and bear arms" must also mean or implies "individual self-defense" or, "defense of themselves" or "defense of him", etc. The nine states that Justice Scalia mentions in his opinion are Pennsylvania, Vermont, Kentucky, Ohio, Indiana, Mississippi, Alabama, Connecticut and Missouri. This selected group of states opens more room for criticism of the majority opinion.

Only two of these states were of the original thirteen states (Pa. and Conn.). Only one, Pennsylvania, had a written constitution *before* the United States Constitution and the Bill of Rights was written, debated upon and ratified. The State of Connecticut (arguably the most conservative state in the union at the time) did not ratify a written state constitution until 1818. Eight of the states noted in Scalia's footnote #8 were frontier states in total or in significant part (Pa.); six of which were located west of the Allegany Mountains and definitely were far more hostile territories than the eastern seaboard states. Self-defense in these frontier states was an essential survival requirement. Also, one must keep in mind that by 1820, which is the year that the justice designates as the end of his selection era there were 24 states in the union. Justice Scalia states:

> "In numerous instances "bear arms" was unambiguously used to refer to the carrying of weapons outside of an organized militia. The most prominent examples are those most relevant to the Second

---

[8] See Stevens' dissent, page 31. Blackstone counsels: "the fairest and most rational method to interpret the will of the legislator is **by exploring his intentions** at the time when the law was made, by *signs* the most natural and probable."

Amendment: Nine state constitutional provisions written in the 18th century or the first two decades of the 19th, which enshrined the right to "bear arms in defense of themselves and the state" or "bear arms in defense of himself (sic) and the state".

Justice Scalia picks only nine out of the twenty-four existing states and only one with a constitution written *prior* to the United States Constitution and Bill of Rights? This suggests that Justice Scalia takes liberty to "cherry pick" 38% of the existing body of states whose constitutional language or absence of language, as in the case of Pennsylvania, that may support his thesis. But do they?

One can argue that the inclusion of the "in defense of themselves" or "in defense of himself" (sic) was deliberately written in these state constitutions *because* defense of "self" was *silent* in the United States Constitution and the Bill of Rights. (See my comment several paragraphs above.) When the state constitutional conventions examined the United States' Bill of Rights in preparation of their respective state constitutions and realized that the federal document was silent on this issue of "self-defense, the state constitutional conventions were motivated to exercise their *Tenth Amendment right*:

"The powers not delegated to the United States by the Constitution, nor prohibited by it to the States, are reserved to the States respectively, or to the people."

The state convention delegates would have felt compelled to incorporate self-defense verbiage in their state documents because of the hostile environments of their territories and the practice of homesteading in isolation from the community of the frontier families. The state conventions included defense of "self" in their state constitutions as a *result* of the federal *silence* on the matter, *not to verbalize an implication* in the federal document. In essence, the Second Amendment of the federal Bill of Rights guarantees the right of the state to have a "well regulated militia" to secure a free state from the tyrannies of an abusive central government and deliberately leaves silent the right for other purposes/uses of arms to be regulated by the states governments that are better equipped by proximity to determine the needs of the local populace in keeping and bearing arms. In summery, the several state constitutions are left free to extend the right for self-defense, hunting or sport shooting as required within the scope of safety and within state boundaries or state circumstances, such as urbanization, hostile indigenous tribes, isolated rural homesteading, wilderness dangers, etc. But in no way, would responsible community authorities neglect the importance of "well-regulated" in the keeping, bearing, handling, or owning firearms for whatever reasons they include for the protections of the citizenry. This makes sense.

The most widely cited decision by the United States Supreme Court on this matter is *United States v. Miller (1939)* that restricts certain firearms to citizens other than militia participants but it falls far short of total abolition of firearms to the general population. This decision (*United States v. Miller*) centered on the use of a "sawed-off shotgun" but over the years was extended to include machine guns (fully-automatic weapons), bazooka/RPG, cannon and assault rifles. Due to the Court's naiveté regarding military weaponry, the Court ruled that individuals in the general population could rely on the Second Amendment to justify the keeping of regular length shotguns (over eighteen inches in length), rifles (but not assault rifles) and handguns or in their words "such arms as a member of the militia might use". This phrase muddled the argument and this innocence on the part of the Court provides for the argument to continue. The issue is that in modern wars the military and, therefore, the established militia use short-barreled shotguns and even long range sporting rifles for their snipers, as well as RPG's, machine guns, automatic assault rifles, etc. This convoluted verbiage in *Miller* actually nullifies the decision in the minds of the gun enthusiasts as a basis for restricting the types of weapons that can be made available to the individual in the general public. Fortunately, the decision has withstood interpretative attack to a great extent and has successfully limited bazookas, RPGs and modern cannon from the streets, most likely because the courts refuse to hear arguments on the illogic of the verbiage in *Miller*. (It is interesting to note, however, that one can purchase Civil War Napoleon Six-pounder cannon for about $6,000 each and have them delivered to his door, even in California.) Hopefully, *Miller* will continue to withstand the onslaught of the gun lobbies that have already threatened to challenge state and local gun restrictions based on the Supreme Court's most recent opinion.

As a matter of fact, the flood gates of criticism were opened and the NRA was not impressed on June 27, 2008 with Justice Scalia's public "side bar" finger waggle in the face of the citizenry to discourage challenges to existing law based on his majority opinion. Wayne La Pierre, Executive Vice-President and CEO of the NRA, immediately challenged Justice Scalia by responding that the gun lobbies would be petitioning every court in the land that attempted to negate the potency of this decision on the basis of the justice's "side bar" warnings. At this very moment the gun lobbies are drafting their petitions!

Machine guns (fully-automatic weapons) are a huge social matter in urban America. These weapons have no sporting value whatsoever but are, unfortunately, readily available, although due to *Miller*, they cannot be legally sold to the general public by licensed gun dealers. They are, however, a weapon of choice of gangs, drug cartels and home invaders. They give the criminal superior firepower over the innocent civilian and even many local law enforcement agencies. Some of these weapons are small and lightweight and can be smuggled into this country much like the illegal drugs that arrive on our streets due to our inept Immigration Service and porous borders. (As a relevant side note, however, the Mexican government complains that most of the illegal weapons that the drug cartels use in that country are, in fact, smuggled *from* the United States.) Of greater danger to the public but closely related to fully-automatic weapons and exacerbating this issue is the relative ease that a *semi-automatic* weapon can be converted to a *fully-automatic* weapon. Only a couple of parts in a semi-automatic weapon need a simple modification to complete the conversion to fully-automatic. However, semi-automatic weapons *are legal* to be sold in the United States. And I might add, that a great many of them, particularly semi-automatic handguns, *are* sold in this country. These are the weapons that cause a very high percentage of the carnage on our streets! Doesn't it just make sense that if the US Second Amendment was written for self-defense of the individual citizen, then the law abiding citizenry should be permitted to "keep and bear" automatic weapons and, perhaps, RPG's, etc. to protect against the criminal element in society in addition to being prepared to respond to the tyrannies of a federal government. Therefore, *Miller* needs to be revisited with this recent decision.

In another sense one could establish that the basic document of the US Constitution used nouns in a collective sense, but in the Bill of Rights these same collective nouns could and still do refer to individual rights. For example, the First Amendment guarantees the rights of *individuals* (?) to free choice and practice of religion, the freedom of speech, or of the press, or the right of the *people* to peaceably assemble, and to petition the Government for a redress of grievances. This amendment has always been interpreted to refer to individuals, even though the singular noun "individual" is omitted from the text, in all of the freedoms listed, *and* to groups (people) *or* to a single individual to peaceably assemble and petition for redress of grievances. The Second Amendment uses only the collective noun "people" but many, and now the current United States Supreme Court in June 2008 interpret this amendment to refer to an individual right. However, the Third Amendment uses the singular noun "Owner". The Fourth uses collective nouns but clearly refers to individual rights. The Fifth uses singular nouns and the Sixth uses a "neutral" noun (that is not either collective or singular) but uses singular pronouns. As one can see, to establish conclusively by linguistic technicality that a right, as expressed in the United States Bill of Rights, is collective or individual is very difficult, if not impossible.

Justice Scalia's recent opinion weighs much too heavily, however, on the linguistics of the Second Amendment, and significantly diminishes the historiography involved in the evolution of this civil right[9]. He cavalierly dismisses 48% of the Amendment and states that 20th century linguistics renders the verbiage superfluous. The justice conveniently ignores James Madison's experiences in collaborating with Thomas Jefferson and George Mason in the development of the Virginia Constitution and its associated Declaration of Rights in 1776 and devotes his energies on the Pennsylvania Constitution that was influenced by the pacifist Religious Society of Friends. The Virginia Declaration of Rights clearly calls for a well-regulated militia formed from the collective members of the community, whether they are members of the body politic or not, to defend against the abuses that the American colonies had suffered under George III. Another principal

---

[9] See Stevens' dissent page 31. Blackstone: "If words happen to be still dubious, we may establish their meaning from the context; with which it may be of singular use to compare a word, or a sentence, whenever they are ambiguous, equivocal or intricate. Thus, the proem, or preamble, is often called in to help the construction of an act of parliament".

point in the majority opinion that does not stand on firm historical footing is the Justice's "circular" argument that nine of twenty-four state constitutions written during the period between 1790 and 1820 included self-defense in the "keep and bear arms" clauses; therefore, the federal Second Amendment must "imply" self-defense and therefore "imply" an individual's right to keep and bear arms. How can documents written after the fact imply meaning to the document in question? Moreover, the drafters of the nine state constitutions mentioned in the majority opinion had no need for an "implied" validation from the federal Second Amendment to include self-dense of the individual in their respective constitutions because they stood on their right under the federal Tenth Amendment that what powers were not delegated or prohibited by the federal constitution were reserved to the States. Furthermore, the majority opinion fails to give proper hearing to the other state constitutions that were written and/or in existence in the time period arbitrarily established by Justice Scalia for the purpose of his position on this matter. These several state constitutions certainly weaken the majority opinion's argument.[10]

Scalia's rhetoric minimizes the passages in Madison's Federalist Papers #46 that clearly argue for a militia "officered by men chosen from among "themselves" (sic)..., is the best defense against a tyrannical central government. A militia so assigned for the defense of the people against the tyranny ascribed in this treatise is not, under any stretch of the imagination, an unregulated, untrained to the manual of arms, mob of squirrel hunters, armed with small bore rifles or shotguns. One needs only to study tactics and strategies of the early wars up to and including the American Civil War to understand the significance of capturing militia/military armories and arsenals to initiate and sustain armed resistance against an abusive despotic government. An armed citizenry, yes, but a citizenry regulated, trained in the manual of arms and supervised by officers with noted community responsibility! A further perusal of the document confirms that Madison's discourse in Federalist Papers #46 did not imply unregulated gun ownership and in no way suggests self-defense as a reason for keeping and bearing arms.

Finally, one has to keep in mind that most state constitutions and the Articles of Confederation were drafted, debated and resolved during

---

[10] See Stevens' dissent opinion ET. Al.

a time of war (1776-1783) with the tyrannical English Royal Government. Contrary to Justice Scalia's assertion that private hunting weapons and combat firearms were identical, careful historical examination begs to differ. Even in the Eighteenth Century combat weaponry differed from sporting/hunting arms. Combat weapons were very sturdy and heavy (nine pounds) so that they could withstand the abuses of the campaign. The combat weapon had the accommodation for a bayonet and a sling. The bayonet was a very important fixture in the era of the single-shot, muzzle-loaded, smoothbore, large caliber (.75 caliber or more) musket. On the other hand, sporting/hunting weapons were often pieces of art; carefully crafted to fit the desires of the shooter. The most well known and widely used was the Pennsylvania Rifle, later designated the Kentucky Rifle. This piece was indeed a work of art. It had a rifled barrel, longer than the military weapon. It was smaller caliber (.50 or less) with a slender, almost delicate stock and weighed only seven pounds. There was no accommodation for a bayonet nor were the weapons made sturdy enough to survive battlefield abuses. Hunting weapons simply were not adequate for soldiering in 1789, in 1861 and certainly are not in this 21st Century of high technology. It is difficult for me to accept that the concerned and educated leaders of the Rebellion would focus on the rights of the citizen to bear arms for self defense, squirrel hunting and fowling in the event that they have to muster to the community's defense during this critical period in history. Combat weaponry had to be foremost in their minds when the American leaders debated how best to protect the citizenry from hostile forces.

I cannot permit myself to leave this thesis without commenting on Justice Scalia's tortured syntax in his writing and his intimidating demeanor directed toward his colleagues on the bench in reasoned discussion. The justice takes sixty-six pages to present his case, but in the process omits some very significant documents that could be viewed as contrary to his arguments; disregards some words and phrasing that could weaken his argument and fails to research the letters, diaries and/or notes of Madison, Adams, Franklin, Jefferson and Mason written during those many months that they struggled with the composition of the Virginia Constitution and its Declaration of Rights and later the

United States Constitution[11]. He relies too heavily on linguistic technicalities at the expense of substantive historiography. Furthermore in my opinion, Justice Scalia distorts the writings of Blackstone for his own conclusions and ignores Blackstone's comments regarding the legitimate process of intrinsic interpretation.

The justice's demeanor is evident throughout his thesis by his use of inflammatory adjectives, other words or phrases that have no import except to denigrate his colleagues on the bench, friend of the court or concerned citizen. Such phrasing as "dead wrong", "bizarre" argument, "profoundly" mistaken, "absolutely" no evidence, "bordering on the frivolous", "an absurdity", "grotesque", "this side of the looking glass", "is worthy of the mad hatter", ad nauseam, are examples of this verbal bullying. (I deliberately used the inflammatory word "absurd" in the second paragraph of this essay as a rebuke to Justice Scalia's style.) Now, I am sure that the other justices, particularly those in the dissenting group don't need any support from some unknown Joe Ordinary, such as me, on this matter. But this type of language either used in conversation or in written form tends to suppress creative thought. I always think of the judiciary as a forum to seek truth, not necessarily the win. And truth needs creative thought. In over thirty-five years divided between the regular military, the active federal reserves and civilian corporate administration, I found that overbearing, intimidating, condescending language clouds issues, denies creative thought and establishes hostile environments. Justice Scalia's intellectual manners in his writings and his oral briefs induce this caustic situation. I believe that in spite of equally intelligent peers on the bench much creative thinking has been stifled due to this abrasive persona. In the collegial environment such as the United States Supreme Court where the intellectual matters of the government are discussed, this abusive conduct is counterproductive.

Even with this decision no viable solution emerges. But Justice Scalia's sixty-six pages of opinion open a Pandora's Box for new arguments regarding the availability of deadly weapons that endanger the public safety. For example: Does the Second Amendment apply to

---

[11] Thomas Jefferson was in France at the time that Madison was authoring the constitution but he and Madison carried on a vigorous communication the included written conversations on the drafting of the United States Constitution. Jefferson did not return to the United States from France until November 1789.

the District of Columbia? Does *this decision* apply *only* to the District? Once again, we hit a "bump in the road" to resolution. The District of Columbia and its domiciles have been pushed and pulled hither and thither like a redheaded stepchild with the itch to find the proper local government protocol. What is its status at this moment and will it remain as is in the future? Is this ruling narrowly defined to the District of Columbia or to all federal government lands such as national parks, forests, military reservations, Indian reservations, federal rivers etc? Will this decision apply to the states, territories and trusts too?

Where did the justice derive "home" as the legal venue for a citizen to own and carry a loaded, unsecured firearm? Home is not mentioned in any of the historical literature that I have ever read. The most notable passages of the pioneers protecting self and family are scenarios of carrying loaded muskets (not handguns) to the fields in the event of ambuscade by indigenous hostiles or carrying the Pennsylvania/Kentucky rifle (never a pistol) on the trek through the Cumberland Gap, or, the reference of a frontiersman who carries his loaded weapon to the community stockade to serve as a militiaman in times of danger. Obviously, these long guns were in the cabins and homes too, but the greatest danger of attack by the indigenous peoples was outside the cabins, stockades or any defensive position for that matter. So, what are the boundaries of "home"? Is it the outer walls of the residence? Is a connected garage a part of the home? What about a detached garage or free standing barn or shed on the property as an extension of the legal venue to carry a loaded firearm? Is the citizen permitted to carry his loaded weapon to the verges of his property? Ambiguity still abounds.

This debate regarding the meaning of the Second Amendment has been going on for a very long time and each session of historical/political/legal rhetoric on this subject seems to do nothing more than deepen and broaden the schism between the left and right. Is it all to no avail? Meanwhile, Columbine happens, Virginia Tech happens, deadly home invasions happen, gang shoot-outs happen, the Larry Kings[12] die, shooting accidents happen, organized crime shoots happen, assassinations happen. Side bar finger waggles have never curtailed ir-

---

[12] This reference is to fifteen year old Larry King, who declared his homosexuality and was shot in the head in the classroom by a classmate.

responsible actions of individuals in this society. I think some prudent wisdom can prevail, however, upon which both the left and the right can rest their cases on this matter and then focus on some other issues that are really far more dangerous to our continued existence on this earth. Let me take a couple of moments of your time to list a few options that should be reviewed, decided upon and implemented:

- Our legislatures (Federal and State as required by the Constitution) can amend the US Constitution's Second Amendment language to include the necessary protections for a well regulated militia *and* a well regulated citizenry to keep/ own and bear arms for the purposes of the security of a free state and the right to self-defense and sportsmanship.

- Or our legislatures (Federal and State as required by the Constitution) can amend the US Constitution with a Twenty-Seventh Amendment to guarantee ownership of *certain* arms to a *well regulated citizenry* for the purpose of self-defense and sportsmanship and leave the Second Amendment to guarantee the right for a well regulated militia for defense from a tyrannical central government.

- Or at the very least the US Supreme Court can expand on the 1939 decision *United States v. Miller* to include semi-automatic weapons as a machine gun and define the term "*well regulated*" of the existing Second Amendment to require proper licensing of all citizens owning firearms, to require proper and thorough training on the use and knowledge of the dangers to the community, to require a rigid psychological screening of any citizen wishing to purchase a firearm and to require that certain citizens due to mental illness or felony conviction be prevented from owning, keeping or bearing a firearm.

Will any of these suggestions eliminate the carnage that this country experiences every year from the illicit use of firearms? Not on your life! However, I think that the proposals listed above or other even better ones that can be implemented will certainly reduce the number of fatalities due to the misuse and the illicit use of firearms.

The goal, of course, is not only to significantly reduce the cost (in lives) but also to preserve a most revered liberty of the citizenry. This cannot happen by one philosophical faction strong-arming the contrary philosophical factions. *There must be accommodation!* The country needs the right wing to buy into this drive to increase the safety of the populace from improper use of firearms. The National Rifle Association can make a significant contribution in this matter. The NRA has the best program to adequately train citizens in firearm safety. They have the best facilities to complete such training. They sanction activities that are *well regulated* for gun enthusiasts to compete in sport shooting. When the Virginia Tech tragedy splashed across the media, Mr. La Pierre, EVP and CEO of the NRA, chastised the bureaucracies for their failures in communicating that the perpetrator did not meet even our present requirements for mental stability to purchase a firearm. This was a very legitimate criticism! The organization has lived (perhaps not comfortably, however) with *United States v. Miller* for 68 years now. The NRA may very well have some good ideas for new language in the US Constitution to protect the *"right"* of the citizens *"to own and bear arms"*. Furthermore, the NRA is entrenched in the right-wing and this organization has a strong influence on the state and federal governments. This organization is crucial for success!

On the other hand, we need the liberal wing to "get real" regarding privacy rights, specifically the communication of mental health records. The safety of the populace is at stake in this matter and some compromise must be devised so that mentally ill people, who have illusions of harming themselves or others, like felons, are not permitted to own or have access to firearms. (It sounds cruel to place destructively ill people with convicted felons, and I don't mean to have it sound that way.) I think that proper protocols can be devised to separate the two groups, but at the same time prevent both groups access to firearms.

Finally, we must find a means to increase the efficiencies of and the communications between the many federal, state and local bureaucracies. Our bureaucracies are appallingly inept! There are bureaucratic fiefdoms all up the public ladder that control authority and jealously protect that turf from other organizations at the expense of their fiduciary responsibilities to the citizenry. Government employees must start working hard *and* smart for the general welfare. It is their job to find a means to protect the privacy of the mentally ill, but at the same time provide an effective means to communicate certain patients' limitations as related to "keeping and bearing" firearms. This will take significant creativity, diligence and efficacy. **But it must be done!**

<u>A NOTE TO THE EXTREMIST RIGHT</u>

(The truth to set the record straight)

During the last seven and a half years the Republican leadership, heavily influenced by extremists to the right, has perpetrated some of the greatest disasters on this country since the beginning of American history.

1. Bush/Cheney started in 2001 with a $279 billion budget surplus and turned it into a $400 billion deficit in eight months by giving the **wealthiest 3%** of the population over **80%** of a $1.38 trillion tax cut. The US National Debt has increased by $300-$400 billion for every year of the Bush/Cheney Administration. Why? Because the Bush/Cheney Administration only did **half** of the job; **they didn't cut expenses.** In fact, they have **increased** expenses to cover an ill-conceived war and have given no-bid contracts to favored politicos.

2. When the Republicans took office the national debt was **$5.7 trillion.** By 2008 it stood at **$9.4 trillion** with an expected addition of $700 billion by the end of this fiscal year. This increase amounts to a **77% increase** in debt in less than eight years! The tax cut was supposed to stimulate a sluggish economy. However, in seven years the GDP has **increased only 30%** while the national debt has **soared 77%!**

3. Bush/Cheney dropped out of the Kyoto Protocols that was designed to address the issues of the global warming by greenhouse gases. Today, every authoritative scientist in the world agrees that the earth is warming and that industrial greenhouse gas emissions are a significant contributor to

the dilemma. Now, even Bush concedes to this world crisis. (Cheney still refuses to pull his head out of the sand.)

4. Bush/Cheney responded to 9/11 with an invasion of Afghanistan with the help of the Northern Alliance. This was a good decision. This coalition temporarily defeated the Taliban and sent the al-Qaeda scurrying to the mountains. But then Bush/Cheney abandoned this war in mid-phase and focused on Iraq. **This was a bad decision.**

5. Bush/Cheney opted for a preemptive invasion of a sovereign nation-state (Iraq) based on spurious intelligence and short of two weeks before the international weapons inspectors concluded their final efforts in the search for WMD's. However, even then the international inspectors were very dubious of any viable WMD stockpile or manufacturing capability in Iraq. No stockpiles or WMD manufacturing capability were ever found in Iraq because they didn't exist.

6. Bush/Cheney misled the congress and the American people with lies that Saddam was harboring al-Qaeda in Iraq and supporting them in their terrorist activities. This has proved to be untrue. As a fact, Saddam Hussein was fearful of the fundamentalist Muslim sects because Iraq was a secular Muslim country.

7. Bush/Cheney ordered the preemptive attack on Iraq with a force that was contrary with the good judgment of the US military leadership. If a military leader had any different view, he/she was forced to resign.

8. Bush/Cheney declared that the Iraq war had reached its final stage only six weeks after the invasion under a banner "MISSION ACCOMPLISHED". Our casualties were light; 139 killed and 542 wounded. However, there were 7,409 non-combatant old people, women and children killed (or murdered?) by collateral destruction. This happened by May 1, 2003.

9. Since the Bush/Cheney declaration of the end of "major combat", the following has taken place in Iraq:
   • US Troops/US civilian contractor/coalition armed forces that have been killed equals: 4093 US Troops + 1200

civilian contractors + 309 coalition combatants = **5602**.

- US Troops wounded in Iraq now equals **28,661**; Civilian contractors filing claims for disabling wounds now equals **12,000**. Combined this equals **40,661**.
- Iraqi noncombatants, such as old people, women and children, killed (or slaughtered or murdered?) by collateral destruction now total over **700,000 souls**[13]. Over **1,000,000 private homes** destroyed and over **4,000,000 souls** have been displaced.
- The US Military lost complete control in the aftermath of the "major combat" period and the entire country fell into total chaos. The looting was staggering; priceless world treasures were stolen or vandalized because there were not enough US "boots on the ground" to control the situation.
- Before the invasion General Eric Shinseki told the administration that we could beat Saddam's army in a few weeks with 150,000 troops but it would take 360,000 to win the peace and prevent the country from falling into chaos. The administration fired General Shinseki, invaded with 160,000 troops, and destroyed only part of Saddam's army in three to four weeks. Iraq immediately fell into chaos and a surviving nucleus of the Ba'ath Party military leadership and rank and file emerged as guerrilla/ insurgents.
- The United States captured and tried Saddam in a Kangaroo Court, declared him guilty of executing 124 conspirators of an attempt of his own assassination (This is a sovereign Head of State prerogative, incidentally) and executed him. How does this crime stack up to the **700,000 plus innocents** that the United States has slaughtered with an ill-conceived preemptive attack with no intrinsic justification?
- Water and electrical utilities in Iraq have not returned to pre-invasion levels; not by a long shot!

---

[13] These are iraqbodycount.org statistics. The Bush/Cheney Administration admits to only **200,000** or more slaughtered. Other less bias organizations put the total between **600,000 and 800,000** slaughtered.

- Bush/Cheney (and company) declared that the war in Iraq would cost no more than **$60 billion**, paid for by cheap Iraqi oil receipts. So far the war has cost over **$600 billion of US taxpayer money** with nary a hint of cheap Iraqi oil footing the bill. Economists are estimating that this war will eventually cost between $2 trillion and $3 trillion. Of this $600 billion plus that the Bush/Cheney gang already has spent in Iraq, $147 billion is unaccounted for! (Now there's some real management oversight for you.)

- Meanwhile, the successful war in Afghanistan has turned south on us. Osama is still on the loose; al-Qaeda has regrouped, recovered and rearmed in the Border Mountains and the Taliban has taken back over 50% of the country. The opium crop and exports have broken all previous records and most of the profits are financing the terrorists. The US backed Afghan government is struggling for control and support is quickly slipping away.

- In Pakistan President Pervez Musharraf resigned from office to avoid impeachment proceedings. Our strongest ally in the Middle East against the global war on terrorists is finished. For seven years this administration has received volumes of evidence that Musharraf's influence was waning in the region, but it continued to pour billions of dollars of support money into his government. In spite of the expense, Musharraf has proved to be of very limited reliability. The Pakistan mountainous frontier with Afghanistan remains a safe haven for al-Qaeda rejuvenation.

- In 2008 our military services are stretched to the breaking point due to multiple troop rotations to the combat zones in the two wars. Our combat equipment is worn out and has not been replaced. Furthermore, our troops are being neglected when they are wounded and sent home. The Walter Reed debacle is one of the most disgusting incidents is all military history.

- Also, our troops often go undiagnosed for PTSD and symptoms are viewed as misbehavior; the suffering soldier is treated as a delinquent, given a general or dishonorable discharge and denied medical benefits from the Veteran's Administration.

- In another deplorable scenario, recently a brigade of soldiers finished an extended tour in Iraq and went home to Fort Bragg, their Zone Interior garrison a couple of months ago. They found their barracks flooded with several inches of water and toxic mold covering the walls. The home station had plenty of notice that this unit was returning to the garrison but no one even bothered to check out their barracks for livability! Is this any way to treat our troops! Some sorry a—general, and, perhaps, some of his underlings need to be fired!

10. Let's review a bit of "Brownie's 'heck of' a job" as director of FEMA. As the American citizenry in New Orleans and along the Gulf Coast were drowning by the hundreds and people were driven from their homes by the tens of thousands, the director of FEMA's spokesperson turned away frantic phone calls for help because Director Brown was eating dinner. Now "Brownie", as he was referenced by President Bush, had an extensive background in Thoroughbred horses so it seems obvious to any of us fools who pay the tax bills that this background qualified him for disaster preparedness and response. Where is that turnip truck?

- Over a **1,000** people died in the Katrina disaster. Over **100,000** people lost their homes. **Billions of dollars** in property values were swept away.
- New Orleans, arguably one of the magnificent historical communities in the USA, was virtually destroyed and **four years later** it still has not recovered and may never recover. Portions of Mississippi also may never recover. There are still thousands of people homeless due to mismanagement of government activities.
- Hundreds of millions of dollars were wasted on trailers that were condemned for human habitation because chemical toxicity.
- The Federal Government's dramatically slow response to its own citizenry has been appalling!

11. Let's take a look at the Bush Administration's attack on the United States Constitution and the Bill of Rights that was designed to protect the citizenry from the tyranny of autocratic controls and abuses. The Patriot Act passed a Republican controlled congress and it immediately placed in jeopardy the protection of the First, Fourth, Fifth and Sixth Amendments of the Bill of Rights for all US Citizens and trashed the Privilege of the Writ of Habeas Corpus.

12. The reputation of the United States in the eyes of the entire world has been sullied by the appalling disregard of our obligations under the Geneva Accords relating to the extraordinary renditions, torture of POWs, foreign combat detainees and US citizens that this administration has perpetrated on thousands of people.

13. The Guantanamo Bay detention/torture facility and the "secret CIA torture centers" are reminiscent of the Holocaust. The Cuban facility has housed up to and over 650 "detainees". Some 300 detainees were released when the abuses at Abu Ghraib prison were revealed to the world. These detainees were never charged with a single criminal act, but were incarcerated for years on hearsay from paid informants. Today, over **270 remain** incarcerated, but only nineteen have been charged with anything that remotely approaches terrorism. These people have been involuntarily detained for over **six years**! On June 12, 2008, however, the United States Supreme Court, arguably the most conservative court in United States history, **struck down** the provision of the **Military Commissions Act of 2006** that allowed for this egregious attack on very basic human rights by the Bush/Cheney Administration. Even the conservatives of the court can't stomach the abuses of the Bush/Cheney regime.

14. The US economy is in a near death spiral.
    - Gasoline prices have increased from $1.53/gal to $4.60/gal during this administration. The oil giants are breaking all profit records, oil industry CEO's are receiving outrageously rich compensations and **the US Government is giving subsidies to these corporations (?)!** However,

no new refineries have been built for over 30 years, and no alternative fuels have been developed, except corn ethanol that needs more energy to produce than it provides for the consumer's automobile. Other more efficient renewable source crops are available such as sugar cane (7 times more efficient), sweet sorghum (5 times more efficient) and even native buffalo grass (2 times more efficient) that is indigenous to our Great Plains. There are probably dozens of other source crops that are more adaptable than corn for ethanol production.

- We also need to invest in clean coal, an economical shale-oil extraction process, more photovoltaic technology, hydrogen fuel technologies, nuclear energy technologies, wind energy technologies and hydro energy technologies. We need leaders who can corral the bickering and focus the several levels of government on solutions. Bush and Cheney have failed to pick up the challenge and have instead feathered the beds of their old school industrialist friends.

- Because of the rise in gasoline prices, food prices are increasing at an alarming rate both here in the United States and throughout the world.

- The housing/mortgage/credit markets are a shambles because this administration doesn't do anything to regulate the free-for-all. They stand by and let the Free Market run its course. Let's be truthful to ourselves, due to human greed, a **free market** scenario (That is, there is no regulation at all.) is akin to a sandlot game with no rules; it's all rough and tumble and the little guys get hurt and can't play anymore and the big guys eventually kill each other off until only one is left standing. A truly free market is a utopian dream and cannot work in the real world.

- Due to pressures from a soaring national debt, the declining value of the US dollar has exacerbated the prices on energy.

- Inflation is quickly getting a strangle-hold on the US economy.

147

- Some neo-cons worry about war with China; it is one of our "most favored nation" trade partners, incidentally. There's no chance of war with this country, the Chinese could just call in the $400 billion plus of loans that they hold over us and bring us to our knees. The United States is up to its ears in debt from the irresponsible tax cuts *and* excessive spending and the Bush/Cheney people don't care a hoot. They will just quietly move back to Texas and leave the mess for the next administration and the American middle class to clean up.

15. We can't forget the debacle labeled "No Child Left Behind". All public schools have been required to extensively test the children so that all can read, write and do arithmetic in a reasonable time period. The tests are designed to evaluate schools and teacher competence as well. This isn't so bad, except that all of the testing has taken away from real learning. I am just waiting for the revelation of a freshman college student that answers a serious discussion question such as "Discuss the pros and cons of *Roe v. Wade* on modern American culture." Our young scholar answers with simply a letter "**A, B, C or D**". "No Child Left Behind" is only half of the solution; the American citizen deserves the whole solution.

16. The Valerie Plame scandal is another example of the egregious abuse of power exhibited by the Bush/Cheney Administration. The law is very clear that the actions by the executive gang were felonious. The public record shows cover-up and stone-walling at the highest levels. At least one and perhaps dozens of our covert operatives were endangered or even killed by this executive behavior. And yet, the one man who took the fall for the other miscreants did not spend a day behind bars. The United States is based on law, and time and again it has been reiterated that the Executive Branch or any branch of government is **not** above the law.

Well, I'll just keep adding to this list about my concerns with the extremists controlling the Republican Party. Something outrageous seems to come on a daily basis.

Regards,

P.S. Tom Cole, Chairman of the National Republican Congressional Committee: Your committee owes me a copy of the results of the survey that I diligently completed several weeks ago. I sent you the processing fee and you replied that you had diverted this $11.00 to the contributions fund. This action was contrary to my directions. This $11.00 was to be used **only** for processing my survey participation. If you can't send me a copy of the results of your survey, please return my $11.00.

Thanks for your consideration in this matter
TMB

www.ingramcontent.com/pod-product-compliance
Lightning Source LLC
Chambersburg PA
CBHW031323290526
45784CB00014B/853